PRAISE FOR MIKE MICHALOWICZ'S BOOKS:

Author's Note: It is important to get reviews from your peers, but I believe feedback from people in the trenches—the people who are using the exact methods specified in the books—is the most relevant. Since I like to buck tradition, here are quotes from three of my favorite letters from readers, one for each of my previous books:

PROFIT FIRST

When I read [*Profit First*], I thought you had lost your mind. No way could this work. I kept doing things the way I was. No longer. Early in 2015 I really started following [*Profit First*] as best as I could.

To give you an idea of what this has done for us, at one point early in 2015 our net profit year over year from year to date 2014 versus 2015 was up 1,721.4%. Nope. No typo. I truly am not kidding. We ended 2015 with Net Profit up 335.3% overall.

—**Keith Fear, Balloons Over The Rainbow**
Want to read the entire letter? Go here: http://bit.ly/pfresults

THE PUMPKIN PLAN

I saw your book propped up on a table. I found the title *The Pumpkin Plan* very interesting, but even more interestingly above the title it read: "A simple strategy to grow a remarkable business in any field." I thought to myself, "this guy obviously does not know my field," and bought it because I felt like the title dared me to. I proceeded to my gate, took my seat, started reading, and I was HOOKED!

Thank you, Mike. Your knowledge and book saved me. I no longer call your book *The Pumpkin Plan,* but my "business bible." *TPE* is my business old testament and *PP* is my business new testament. :-) I will continue to follow your books to the letter. I cannot say thanks, or praise you enough for these two books.

—**Andrew Houston, Bookworm English Academy**
Want to read the entire letter? Go here: http://bit.ly/ppresults

THE TOILET PAPER ENTREPRENEUR

The Toilet Paper Entrepreneur is only for those who dream with their eyes open, and dare to make their dreams reality with grit and determination. It stirs and motivates the personality I possess, and speaks to the path I've followed. In that respect it is validation; encouragement for all of us who avoid the beaten track and cut trails of our own, sometimes rebelliously, often obstinately certainly.

—**Cezar, Top 10 Reggae Artist**
Want to read the entire letter? Go here: http://bit.ly/tperesults

If you would like to read professional endorsements for my books, or industry reviews, please visit my website at www.MikeMichalowicz.com.

SURGE

OBSIDIAN
PRESS

SURGE

TIME THE MARKETPLACE, RIDE THE WAVE OF CONSUMER DEMAND AND BECOME YOUR INDUSTRY'S BIG KAHUNA

BY MIKE MICHALOWICZ

Publisher: Obsidian Press
Print Management: Book Lab
Cover Design: Liz Dobrinska
Book Design & Typesetting: Chinook Design, Inc.

2 3 4 5 6 7 8 9 10

ISBN-10: 0981808247
ISBN-13: 978-0981808246

Printed in the United States of America

CONTENTS

For my son, Tyler.
You've caught life's surge.
I can't wait to see how you carve it up.

ACKNOWLEDGMENTS

This book became a reality because the imminent swell was spotted by Lee Strayer. Thanks, Lee, for pointing it out and helping me start paddling.

If there is one person who has put my books in the most hands it is Yaniv Masjedi of Nextiva. You are a wonderful friend and a true class act. Not to mention you and your family know a bit about growing massively successful companies. I have never seen a group of entrepreneurs consistently catch so many surges.

Thanks to Ron Saharyan for promoting the hell out of this book (and all my books), because "people gotta know this shit!" Thanks to Ron (same Ron), Kristina Bolduc, Jackie Letkowski, and Erin Mojer (and the soon to be discovered new talent we invite to join our crazy crew) for running, growing, and maturing our company while I am flying all over the planet talking about this stuff.

A massive outpouring of appreciation and gratitude to Donna Leyens. Donna has been a champion for all my projects for so long and has turned so many people on to my books! I can't wait to see the organization you launch, Donna. And I can't wait to see the book you write. Thank you for allowing me to share your story in *Surge*.

Thank you to the other rock star entrepreneurs, business owners and surfers who shared their stories with me for this book: Holly Beck, Jabe Blanchard, Becky Blanton, Tomas Gorny, Bert Jacobs, Dr. Venus Opal Reese, Paul Scheiter, David Schnurman, Brian Smith and Cyndi Thomason.

Chris Curran, the man who can make anyone's voice velvety, thank you for the powerful support and direction on building a podcast that just plain ol' rocks.

A huge hug of gratitude to Li "Sid" Hayes for helping me get the word out to every nook and cranny on this planet. Plus you have always been a great Big Sid. But you know that.

A major shout-out to all Profit First Professionals. You are a courageous group of folks boldly serving entrepreneurs to grow in so many ways. To me you are the Green Beret of surging profit. You are the force eradicating entrepreneurial poverty.

Thanks to all the "in the trenches" editors who gave me feedback and were willing to be guinea pigs. I am wishing a wonderful surge for all of you: Debra Angilletta of DebraAngilletta.com; Debbie Bilello of Virtual Office Solutions; Michelle Bredell of Account Tally; Karen Dellaripa of Beyond Your Books; Jill Frillman of Bookkeeping Etc.; Billie Anne Grigg of Pocket Protector Bookkeeping; Tina Forsyth, the author and coach at TinaForsyth.com; Peg Hill of Adjusting Entries; Martin Horton of Rivington Accounts Limited; Ann Jewell of Common Cents Books; Jennifer Juguilon-Hottle of J2H Consulting Group; Benita Königbauer of Benita Königbauer Steuerberaterin (Ich danke Dir); Gary Martin of Back To Black Bookkeeping; Susan Penner of Susan Penner Bookkeeping; Kerry Postel of Abacus Bookkeeping, LLC; Janet Redford of MindBlown; Jason Spencer of Spencer Weddings & Entertainment; Dr. Sabrina Starling of Tap the Potential LLC; Derrick "DP" Storey of Derrick P. Storey & Associates Limited; Jillian Verdun of JMV Financial Services; Michele Williams of Scarlet Thread Consulting and Chris Woodard, an entrepreneur and supporter extraordinaire. You are all extraordinary people, and I hope the readers of this book work with you to achieve their surge.

Gracias por mi familia Mexicano–Rodrigo Laddaga, Maru Medina, y Juan Manuel González Ponce. And all thanks to mi familia Americano. Krista, I live you (that is not a typo). Brah, Slaps, and Palzy, I love you.

As always, I tip my hat, my head, and my heart to Anjanette Harper, my co-writer, my friend, and a master of one liners.

Finally and most certainly I want to thank the readers of my books who email me (I hope you will too). I love hearing your stories of success. I love hearing the impact my words and, more importantly, *your* actions, have had on your business and life. I am blown away that *Profit First* has saved so many businesses from financial ruin and saved some marriages in the process (seriously). I am humbled that *The Pumpkin Plan* has played a role in growing so many companies. I can't believe that *The Toilet Paper Entrepreneur* continues to inspire entrepreneurs to take the leap, without a parachute (the only way to successfully leap).

Every morning I read the emails and letters (shout out to the old-schoolers) and videos (shout out to the new-schoolers, too) that you send me. I love hearing how you have fixed, grown, changed, and improved yourselves and your businesses. It touches my soul every time and affirms I am living my life's purpose. Thank you. From the entire essence of my soul, thank you. Email me any day, any time, with your stories at Mike@MikeMichalowicz.com. Old schoolers can mail me at Obsidian Press, ATTN: Mikey M, P.O. Box 73, Mountain Lakes, New Jersey, 07046.

SURGE ON!

"The entrepreneur always searches for change, responds to it, and exploits it as an opportunity."

Paul Drucker

INTRODUCTION

Y OU CAN'T MANUFACTURE LUCK. IT JUST HAPPENS. OR IT doesn't.

For most of my life, I believed that to be true. One morning I'd find a ten-dollar bill on the street and call it a lucky day. A few weeks later I'd realize I lost a twenty somewhere between meetings and call it a crappy day. To be in the right place at the right time, or the wrong place at the wrong time, seemed simply to be a matter of happenstance; it was completely random and out of my control.

Or was it?

A few years ago, Becky Blanton's story came up at one of my Entrepreneurs' Organization (EO) meetings. You may have seen her moving TED talk about being homeless for eighteen months. Her story is powerful and a must-watch, but the discussion at EO was about Becky's unique ability to find lost money on the street. She developed a method based on identifying patterns and, using that method, picked up five to fifty dollars a week. Every week. If I found fifty bucks over the course of a week, I'd think the seas had parted and pigs had learned to fly. Talk about luck, fifty bucks a few weeks in a row would clearly mean I had massive amounts of luck on my side. But for Becky, luck had nothing to do with it. She expected it. She created it.

I started to think about that elusive "good fortune" so many big business success stories seemed to feature. I thought about how, no matter how hard I worked, or how well I networked, or how many books I read (or wrote, for that matter), my current business still wasn't taking off. I'd had success in the past, but not this go-round, and had started to buy into the theory that most entrepreneurs subscribe to: Sometimes you do everything right, and you still can't make your business work. Sometimes you just can't predict the trends that shake up your industry. Sometimes luck is not on your side. Right?

Wrong. I was wrong. *So* wrong.

After hearing Becky's story, I began to change my belief about the concept of luck. What if luck had nothing to do with it? Or—and here is where I began to have a radical thought—what if I could *create* my own luck simply by paying attention to the patterns in my own industry?

Maybe Becky was on to something. Maybe spotting a trend before it took off wasn't a skill exclusive to media darlings and wunderkinder. Maybe I *could* manufacture luck.

In the years since I heard Becky's story, I studied "luck" and applied what I learned to my businesses. Sometimes I failed; sometimes I succeeded. Eventually, I came up with my own method for spotting what others are not trained to see: the next trend in my industry. I figured out how to be in the right place at the right time, over and over again. The more I practiced it, the easier it was to implement. And now that I know my method works, I'm ready to let you in on it.

When I sat down to write this book, I contacted Becky Blanton to ask if she would agree to an interview. I wanted to hear her story firsthand. As luck (ahem) would have it, we were able to meet for breakfast at a Waffle House on the outskirts of Charlottesville, Virginia.

After the death of her father in 2006, Becky packed everything she owned into a 1975 Chevy van and set out to travel the country with her dog and cat. It was a grand idea, but more difficult in practice. Despite her success as a journalist, despite her education and experience, she ended up homeless for more than a year.

2

Though she had a job at a camping store at the time, Becky often went without food for two or three days in a row. In search of enough money for a cheap meal, Becky began looking for money people dropped on the street. "I'd be at Walmart, three dollars to my name, and look around the parking lot for change," she said. "I started thinking, 'Where do I usually find money?' Whenever I found money, I'd notice the things those places had in common. Then I'd ask myself, 'What do those places have in common with *other* places?' Then I would start looking for that pattern in my environment."

Becky noticed she often found money where it could be trapped, usually wherever she could spot a ninety-degree angle. "There's always a corner or a curb. Phone booths. Milk crates lying around are like money butterfly nets. Finding money was like learning the good fishing spots, except I was learning the good money 'catch and hold' spots."

Another pattern Becky discovered yielded her even more cash: She tended to find money in places where people most frequently take bills and coins out of or put money in their pockets, or where money might fall out. "It sounds gross," Becky said, "but people always drop quarters and nickels and dimes around toilets. Nobody wants to dig around on the floor and pick up their own change. People also drop money at bus stops, but don't even notice because they're in a hurry to get on the bus. The clanking of coins is covered by the buses' engine noise, and dollars float away in silence."

Paying attention to this pattern, Becky consistently found money near hot dog vendors and parking meters, in arcades, at bus stops, of course, and—duh—in couches at furniture stores.

"Almost no one sees the money that is constantly around them. But I find dimes, quarters and dollars all the time," Becky said. "You have to train your eyes for it. Once it's on your radar, you do it all day. I still do it, because it's a habit. My friends ask all the time, 'How do you always find money?' I just know what to look for. Once you've seen the pattern, you spot it all the time. You see opportunity everywhere. And once you learn the practice, you can do it anytime, anywhere."

As I dug into my fried eggs and my sweet cream waffle, I thought about the Big Kahunas, the business legends. Every successful business you can think of had a big dose of good fortune; they were at the right place at the right time: AirBNB, Facebook, Uber, Google, Apple, Microsoft, Ford, the company leading in your industry, every single industry leader. Most people would say the founders of

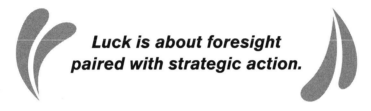

**Luck is about foresight
paired with strategic action.**

these companies got lucky, that opportunity just landed in their laps. Those people would be only half right.

The founders of rock star companies truly were lucky… but I was starting to see that good fortune didn't just fall into their laps. It was a revelation to realize that being in the right place at the right time doesn't have to be some arbitrary force of the universe. Luck isn't about fate, or worth, or karma, or tiny green Irish men. Luck is about foresight paired with strategic action. Luck is about planning. Luck is about deliberately putting yourself in the right spot at the right time. Spot the next trend wave that is almost upon you, position yourself in front of it and you'll capture a surge of consumer demand for your product or service.

I know the prospect of spotting and riding trend waves can seem daunting. It would be so much easier if we could just buy a crystal ball or master time travel. As I was finishing the edits on this, my fourth book and the first in my "Sweet Spot" series, we officially entered the future—the future in *Back to the Future Part II*, that is. When I was but a wee lad, suffering through acne and getting stood up for awkward teenage group dates (I didn't even know that was possible… until it happened), I watched Marty McFly travel to 2015 to save his future son. As an adult, I often wished I had my own DeLorean time machine so I could travel to the future and figure out what the heck consumers want, before they know they want it. It's beyond frustrating to build a business only to have everything come down to happenstance.

Spotting and riding a trend wave might sound about as doable to you as finding your very own DeLorean time machine. I know you're eager for answers. You've done everything you can for your business. You took a risk on your big idea. You worked your butt off, sacrificed your retirement fund and time with your family, and educated yourself about better business practices. You sucked it up and learned how to network. You found your way over, under, or around every challenge that came your way. So why isn't your business the Big Kahuna in your industry? Why is your company still limping along, yet to live up to the potential you envisioned? What will it take for *your* business to experience a powerful surge of consumer demand?

The answer is simple: You have to be in the right place at the right time. (Yes, it all comes back to that essential truth.)

When I give keynote speeches on this topic, this is usually the moment when I hear groans from the audience. I'm always surprised (but grateful) that people don't throw tomatoes at me or rush the stage in an angry mob. I suppose no one lashes out at me because they know I'm right. Anyone who has been in business for a few years knows that no matter how hard you work, or how brilliant your idea is, you haven't got a chance if you haven't accurately anticipated market demand. So why the groans? Because most people believe luck is something out of their control. I did—until Becky Blanton's story inspired me to think differently.

I've been in the entrepreneurial trenches for twenty years now, and if there's one thing I know for sure, it's that conventional wisdom is usually a bunch of B.S. When it comes to business, luck is entirely within your control. I'm sure plenty of people will disagree with me; I'm used to it. I've ruffled a few feathers via my books (one Amazon review of my books hints that I am the devil child, saying, "He's the devil child.") and speeches (I was invited to keynote a CPA conference, and when I said I would explain why profit

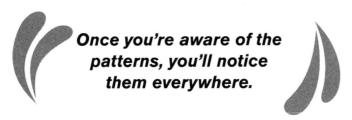

Once you're aware of the patterns, you'll notice them everywhere.

should never be the bottom line, but the top line… I was promptly disinvited). But it is only by busting myths that you successfully build a business. I'm all about doing what works, not what *should* work. I've seen a lot of businesses fail simply because the leaders at the helm followed the status quo without question.

After all these years, I can say with absolute certainty that timing is everything. I built and sold two multimillion-dollar businesses, launched two other successful businesses—including another multimillion-dollar business)—and built a career as an author and speaker. I also had more failures than successes, and after I made ridiculous amounts of money with my companies, *I* became ridiculous and wasted away all my money. But unlike most people, I no longer believe good timing is reserved for "the lucky ones" who stumble upon a once-in-a-lifetime opportunity, or the geniuses who have some "sixth sense" about commerce. Nope. Being in the right place at the right time is a process that anyone can master. As Becky said, you just have to notice the patterns. Once you're aware of the patterns, you'll notice them everywhere.

You might think this is where I tell you that *Surge* will teach you how to build your own DeLorean time machine. I mean, not *really*, but, you know, metaphorically speaking. Nope. You don't need it. The five-step SURGE process I detail in this book will not only teach you the method of identifying the next wave of demand in your business, but also how to capture its energy and ride that wave like a pro.

I don't just write about this stuff. This method isn't merely a concept or a simple derivative of the clarity of hindsight. SURGE is the process I used in my own business. After implementing some of the SURGE techniques, I modified some of what I learned to better meet my own needs and objectives (you should do the same) and boiled the steps down to the simple process I share in this book: the essence of SURGE.

You see, you and I are in the same boat. As I wrote this book, I was deep in the surge of my newest company, Profit First Professionals (PFP). To get PFP off the ground, I made extensive use of the exact SURGE method you are about to learn. Not only did SURGE work for me… it worked *fast*. And it will for you, too.

After I finished my second serving of Waffle House coffee, Becky and I walked out into the parking lot to bid each other adieu. I fumbled for my keys while Becky, almost unnoticeably, scanned the curbs. A crumpled twenty-dollar bill sat right next to the gutter, hidden in plain sight. She picked up the bill, flattened it out, and exclaimed, as she put it in her pocket, "It's gotta be my lucky day… again."

Settle in. You're about to get lucky too.

THE POWER OF WAVES

YOU CAN CALL ME BOB. NO, IT'S NOT MY SECRET GIVEN name. It's not a nickname, either. At least not a *nice* nickname. And it surely isn't my safe word. Here's why *some* people call me Bob:

For the past ten years or so, my December festivities have kicked off with a "Man Day" trip. My mastermind group just happens to be all guys, and together we spend an afternoon doing "manly things":

1. We must shoot some kind of weapon at a target. Last year we shot apples off the heads of plastic zombies with crossbows. (No one actually hit a single apple, just the zombies… because that is the manly way it is supposed to be.)

2. We must compete in some kind of high-speed race. Go-karts, without speed limiters, are usually our go-to choice. Snowmobiles (with speed limiters… we're not that crazy) are a popular alternative.

3. We must only eat meat, with an optional side plate of more meat. One preparation is permitted: rare or don't eat at all.

4. We must end the day smoking a cigar and drinking whiskey. And if you don't like that, you can smoke another cigar and drink another whiskey until you do.

5. And, of course, no feelings are permitted. Not on this day. Not a word.

I have met face to face with these same guys once a month for the past ten years. And while Man Day is the only day in the year we allow ourselves to act like meathead ogres, every other day we meet *is* about feelings. We support each other in the growth of our businesses and in navigating the intricacies of life. These guys have witnessed my transition from selling my companies to becoming full of myself and placing too much importance on my newfound wealth. They watched me lose it all. They have seen me fall to my knees sobbing and have picked me up (figuratively and literally). They helped me become an author. And most recently they have been firsthand witnesses to my most recent struggle… failure to launch. These guys know me better than I know myself. And they know that often, an honest—albeit blunt—observation is far more effective than a kumbaya session.

A couple of years ago, on the morning of Man Day, we each shared a "quick" assessment of our individual businesses before heading out to shoot things. At the time, I was a co-owner in a few businesses. The businesses were all led by amazing people, but for some reason none of them experienced strong, fast growth. All were profitable. All had carved out a niche. All were innovative. But for some reason they weren't sailing forward. I was really frustrated.

Things were okay, but stagnant. I was ready to replicate what I had done with my prior businesses, ready to grow, but for some reason I couldn't get that spark. Something was missing. I thought I had all the answers (which, by the way, is the first indicator that you don't). It is truly demoralizing to be the guy *shouting* from the rooftops—ahem, writing books quietly on airplanes and in the basement—and sharing the steps it takes to grow the business of your dreams, and then failing to do it for yourself.

Just before my turn to speak, I thought, *For God's sake, I write books on this crap, and now look at me. I am standing here with a finger and thumb in the shape of an L for Loser on my forehead.*

"Okay, Mike. You're up."

As I got rolling with my own little State of the Union, my peers inquired about my businesses. They dove into everything I was doing. They asked me about the clients I served. They asked me about my offerings. How about the marketing? How about the specializations? The unique-nesses? The systems?

Then my friend RJ Lewis asked, "Where is the surge?"

"What?" I asked.

"Where is the customer surge, Mike?"

"What are you talking about?"

RJ said, "Where are your customers going? What are they doing, completely regardless of you? What is the biggest change that your customers are dealing with? Where is the surge?"

I ordered a few more pots of coffee for our unexpectedly long session. The zombies were going to have to wait, which, by the way, is the golden rule of Man Day: Nothing is more important than doing whatever it takes to support the other guy, even if that includes cancelling Man Day. I guess Man Day isn't that ogre-ish after all.

RJ went on to explain the surge. In the past five years, the company he launched, Ad-Juster, had become the number one player in "online advertising discrepancy resolution." I don't know what that means either. But I do know he had top-shelf customers flocking to him and a wallet representative of that.

RJ and the guys went on to explain that surge is the force of the marketplace, so powerful that it rolls forward, crushing what is in its path and carrying that which rides on top of it.

A few more hours in and it was clear: picking a niche is critical, but not enough. Serving that niche with singular focus is not enough. Ensuring your business is profitable in that niche is mandatory, but profit surely doesn't ensure growth. There is more to it—the natural direction your niche is moving. Like a massive herd of animals, your customers may be seeking out a new source of food or water or shelter. They may be seeking comfort or fighting for survival. Of course, herds run from things, too. Danger, for example. And so do niches… like the danger of new competition that is wiping them out.

RJ made it clear: My job, your job, our job is to find the surge. Where is your target market headed? Where are they surging? When you find the surge, you can position your company in front of it and ride it all the way to remarkable growth.

"Of course, you could just bob up and down in the marketplace," RJ added. "You could paddle around in circles. You could ignore the waves and instead of riding them, just *bob* up and down. The choice is yours, Bob."

I was floored. Waiting for a response, RJ stared me down. The other guys looked at me and asked, "Where is the surge, Bob?"

TIMING IS EVERYTHING

My Uncle Bill had a favorite joke and he would tell it every time my family visited him. With all of us sitting around the dinner table, Uncle Bill would instruct my father to ask him a specific question: "To what do you attribute your extraordinary comedic talent?" As my Dad started to faithfully recite the question back to Uncle Bill, "To what do you…" Uncle Bill would interrupt mid-sentence and say, "Timing!"

Get it? Timing. LOL.

Uncle Bill was right. Timing is everything. *Everything.*

Let's talk about Skype for a moment. Skype didn't become a massive success because of video conferencing; that technology already existed when the company launched. Skype was in the right place at the right time. It caught the customer surge. "What surge," you ask? The surge of people turning their cameras on themselves.

Skype launched in 2005 as an alternative to making costly international phone calls. Though Skype experienced consistent growth every year, for its first four years in business its customers used a fraction of the billions of minutes burned up on international phone lines. Then, in 2009, the tide turned. Skype-to-Skype customer usage more than doubled that year, and was equal to the number of minutes used in traditional international calls. As in, wait for the tone, then dial 011, the country code and the number, and then wait for that bizarre sounding ringtone on the other side.

So what happened? What caused the surge in Skype's business? In 2006, Apple put a camera into a laptop. The technology to do

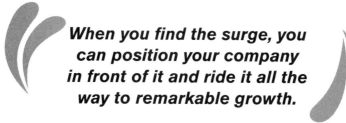

When you find the surge, you can position your company in front of it and ride it all the way to remarkable growth.

this existed before 2006, but at that time, most people had to attach a camera *to* their laptops to use video conferencing. After Apple included a camera in all of their laptops, other laptop manufacturers quickly followed suit. And because laptops have a life span of about three years, by 2009 most people owned laptops with built-in cameras. By 2012, Skype outpaced the growth of the traditional international phone industry. And in 2013, Skype's growth rate was fifty percent higher than all the international phone companies combined.

Skype sold to Microsoft for $8.5 billion. The company's success is in part credited to its technology. No question. But its meteoric rise was due to the fact that it was at the right place at the right time. Skype was primed and ready to take advantage of the built-in camera surge.

Your success is more about timing than anything. Yes, you need to have a great offering that is *distinct* from your competition—that's the "right place" part. And the "right time" is all about catching the marketplace wave as it rolls through. Miss it, and you can paddle all you want and still not be successful. You can't beat the tide. No one can.

If you want to experience stratospheric growth, you need to master timing. You need to intentionally be in the right place at the right time. Will you get it perfect each and every time? No. Most businesses don't, and I certainly didn't. But when you concentrate your efforts to capture the surge, you can greatly improve the odds of achieving colossal success.

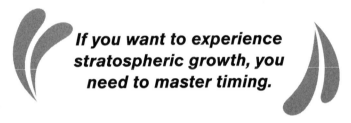

If you want to experience stratospheric growth, you need to master timing.

Timing the market is the Holy Grail of investors, after all. They know that if they can get ahead of the market by a day, by hours or even by a few seconds, there's money to be made. If they can do that repeatedly, there are billions to be made. Brokerage firms spend massive amounts of money to get even a millisecond in timing advantage. My neighbor and poker buddy Scott Dages is the head of IT for one such firm. His team constantly upgrades their connectivity to the trading floor. New fiber, shorter connections, streamlined code, faster servers—everything is improved for efficiency. If new code allows servers to process an order even a millisecond faster, Scott makes the change. Huge money is to be had for Scott and the firm if they constantly work on timing. Huge losses are to be sustained if they ignore it.

Brokerage firms invest in an endless stream of companies and if they get the timing right even a modicum of the time, they make millions. Their method is one way to make money, but you're in a far better position. You don't have to string together a stream of successes. You don't have to time things perfectly over and over. You just need to catch the wave once and you will skyrocket to being your industry's authority. You are not betting on a small portion of someone else's company. You are betting one hundred percent on your company. And the reward for getting the timing right for your own business will put all those brokerage guys to shame.

The founders of Google didn't nail it because their search engine was better, even though some would argue that it was. Google became huge because of timing. Yahoo!, Alta Vista, and other search engines were around before Google, but with the stratospheric volume of content being produced on the web, a growing surge of users were becoming distracted by the web's countless rabbit holes. Yahoo! and other engines were pumping news, email, ads—everything they could get on the screen—distracting users from the little search box. Users of these search engines were frustrated; they simply wanted to find what they were looking for. Google entered the market with a single input box and logo on the screen. It introduced the right solution (a screen with no distractions) at the right time (as people were getting seriously distracted by an overwhelming web and just wanted answers to their question fast). Better search engines have come into existence since Google's rise, but because that wave passed, Google has maintained its position as industry leader.

The founders of Skype didn't have the experience, knowledge, or history to be successful. But they were, and wildly so. Why? Timing. The stratospheric rise of Uber? Timing. The massive success of AirBNB? Timing. Apple? Timing. Ford? Timing. Edison? The master of timing, repeatedly. Wright brothers? Timing. Galileo? Good timing. Copernicus? Better timing. The guy who invented the wheel? Serious timing. Bill Gross's wildly popular TED video explaining why timing is the single biggest reason why startups succeed? He timed talking about timing perfectly. The successful rich guy down the street? Timing. The successful businesses in your industry, on your block, down the hall? Timing. Every successful person you know? Timing.

The success of your business? Timing.

CAPTURING WAVES

Surfers know the importance of timing. Patience is paramount—an inexperienced surfer simply tries to catch the next wave, while an ace surfer patiently waits for the right wave. Of all the factors that come into play in their success—experience, knowledge, and expertise—nothing is as important as timing. As I write this, Garrett McNamara holds the record for the largest wave ever surfed. His 78-foot ride in Nazaré, Portugal is world-famous. But if he had tried to do it a month earlier, or a day later, or simply decided to sleep in that afternoon and head out to the water whenever, that wave wouldn't have been there. He would have missed that massive surge and his chance to break the world record.

You can only ride the biggest marketplace wave when *it* appears. You don't make it happen. And you can't have a killer ride on a ripple. It's impossible. Passion is mandatory. Skills are important, of course. Experience (usually) helps; a history translates into confidence, without a doubt. But all that stuff is useless if you don't have a wave to ride. And all that stuff is insignificant when the wave presents itself.

I was so green when I started my first business that it took a lot of trial and error to finally accept that I likely won't get rich, or happy, or fulfill my purpose on this planet by trying to figure out what's hot and then trying to serve that guess. Thankfully, the SURGE process isn't about *making* waves or watching the ones others are already surfing. SURGE is about *capturing* waves—spotting the imminent market trend that is on the verge of swelling and then riding it all the way to industry domination.

Have you ever gone into a pool with a floatie and bounced around in the water making "waves?" That might be cool for the little kiddies, but nobody is going to surf those waves. Now imagine taking that blow-up floatie of yours into the ocean to bounce around. Making waves in a pool was hard enough; in the ocean it just isn't going to happen. Plus, you'll kind of look like an idiot.

Just as you can't make your own surfable waves in the ocean, you can't create your own waves in the markets. Yeah, you may make that killer app that everyone swarms to, but you didn't make the market wave. That energy was already pent up in the customer base. They were already moving and looking; they just found you because you were in the right place at the right time. You capture waves; you don't make them.

> **SURGE is about capturing waves—spotting the imminent market trend that is on the verge of swelling and then riding it all the way to industry domination.**

Trying to create your own wave is exhausting and just leaves you tired, bobbing around in the same place. Most of us struggle with a day-to-day scramble, seeking new customers and new sales. We exert extraordinary effort prospecting, marketing and selling. Soon enough, it's an all-consuming obsession to get that next client. Then, when that sale does come in, we stop everything else we were doing to exert extraordinary effort delivering on our promises. And then we have little time or energy to sell more or educate the market. The work needs to be done. When the job is complete, the cycle starts anew, and we are desperate to sell again, because the marketplace has dried up. Panic-fueled sales lead to exhausting work, which leads to more panic-fueled sales, and so forth and so on. Sound familiar?

This flip-flopping around in the ocean is our attempt to make our own waves, or an attempt to paddle like mad to catch a wave that has already passed. It is not a mere coincidence that all this desperate splashing and gasping for air looks like drowning, because it basically is. Struggling businesses are always paddling, but seldom get anywhere.

Real, lasting success depends on finding a way to align your company with the natural, powerful waves that are already rolling through the ocean that is your industry, every day. In nature, a wave is a confluence of events: storms and winds, the moon's gravitational pull, even landslides and earthquakes. A wave is really a movement of energy. The water isn't necessarily moving; energy is moving through the water, causing the surface to rise and fall. Because of the way waves form, any surfer will tell you that you need to start paddling in the same direction the wave is moving *before* it arrives, so that you get carried by the momentum of that wave. If you aren't already moving in the right direction when the wave shows up, you're likely to get tumbled or left behind.

In business, waves are also a natural confluence of events: the changing winds—and storms—of customer demand, the gravitational pull of the economy, the industry-shaking quakes caused by advancing technology, and the landslides of collapsing competitors. All of these factors cause waves. As entrepreneurs, our job is to look for these waves as they begin to roll in on the horizon. And if we catch one for the ride of a lifetime, we'd better start paddling like mad in the same direction *before* it arrives.

When I discovered that there is a *process* to catching waves, it occurred to me that surfing was a great analogy for my SURGE process. Surfing waves and catching industries trends is a perfect analogy. First and foremost, surfers always follow these five steps:

1. LOOK—Be on the lookout for swells in the distance and identify those with the most potential.
2. PADDLE—As the swell approaches, paddle in front of it to best match the direction and speed of the wave so that you have the greatest chance for it to carry you. Find the shoulder, the least steep part of the wave and the easiest to ride.

3. **Pop Up**—Feel the wave to first lift you up and then push you. This is the energy of the wave transferring to you and your board. In one smooth move, stop paddling and stand up on the board to ride.

4. **Confirm**—Now that you are standing on the wave, determine if the wave has a pocket. The pocket is the heart of the wave that allows surfers to gain speed and perform maneuvers. Some waves don't have pockets, and surfers are forced to ride the shoulder. If your wave does not have a pocket, it's time to dump it and look for the next. Always look for the wave's pocket and adjust as it moves.

5. **Ride**—Now that you are up on a good wave, there is only one thing left to do: Ride it for all it's worth.

A MASTER CLASS IN SURFING

Arguably, nobody knows how to ride a marketplace wave better than Brian Smith, the founder of the iconic footwear brand UGG. When Brian graciously agreed to be interviewed for this book, I was stoked. His story is legendary. If you know me at all, you know my deal is figuring out how to apply—and sometimes upend—successful business strategies for my own businesses. Then, when I figure out a system and master it for myself, I write a book and teach you how to do it. That's my happy place. Getting a chance to talk extensively with Brian about his massive business success was a huge honor and had me buzzing with excitement throughout our conversation.

As Brian and I spoke, he explained that he grew up surfing the beautiful beaches of his native Australia before becoming an accountant back in the 1970s. He hadn't been an accountant long when he realized that he wanted to do something different. Something *bigger*. He wanted to start his own company, a company that created products he would want to buy. If only he could find a trend to ride with a product that appealed to his surfer lifestyle, he could create a company he would love. And if he got the surge right, so would the rest of the world.

Like any good surfer, Brian started looking to the horizon to see where those new trends, those *waves*, were coming from. He thought about some of the coolest products that appealed to surfers, like waterbeds and Levi's jeans and cutting-edge boards, and he noticed that those things were all coming from California.

"The California surfing scene was my lifestyle, and the products I liked all came out of California," Brian explained. "So I decided that I would go to California to find the next big thing to bring back to Australia." In other words, plant yourself where the waves are forming. Lesson one.

Brian moved to Santa Monica to saturate himself in the California surfer culture and find his product "wave," but even after a couple of months of relentless research he still hadn't hit on anything of interest. Waiting for waves requires patience, persistence and perspective. Lesson *dos*.

Then, on a nondescript day in 1979, Brian's surfing buddy Doug Jensen brought a copy of *Surfer Magazine* with him for a day of riding the waves at Malibu. Brian recalled flipping through the monthly rag: "I got goose bumps. There was an ad for an Australian company, with a picture of this pair of legs wearing sheepskin boots in front of a fireplace, and I thought 'Oh my God, there are no ugg boots in America!'"

Brian spotted a cresting wave heading in a totally different direction than he expected. He wasn't going to bring a hot new product back to Australia as he originally planned. He was going to bring Australia's iconic sheepskin footwear to the United States fashion market. Massive waves initially start as little bumps, far out in the ocean, and aren't necessarily heading in the exact direction you expect. Once you spot your wave, you must never take your eyes off it. Lesson *trois*.

"Doug! Do you see that?" Brian remembered telling his friend. "We're going into business and we're going to be millionaires!" According to Brian, one in two Australians had some type of sheepskin footwear. In Australia, sheepskin shoes were like flip-flops. Everybody had a pair. They called them "uggs."

But the boots also matched a confluence of events in the world of surfing. Surfing was no longer just a summer hobby; it was a year-round sport. Advancements in wetsuits and materials such as neoprene, the rise of competitive surfing for cash prizes, and the fashion-setting standard of the California surfer were all changing the surfing lifestyle. And as part of this changing tide there was a small, yet powerful, wave forming: cold feet. Literally, cold feet. A professional surfer would finish a set in the chilly Pacific Ocean and end up standing on the beach with freezing feet. That distant bump was there; serious American surfers needed something to keep their feet warm and fashionable during cooler surfing months.

Brian scraped together five hundred dollars to buy six pairs of sheepskin boots from the company that ran the magazine ad, and he also got the okay to be their US distributor, six pairs of boots and all. It was time for Brian to start paddling. Lesson *wyoorg*. (That's "four" in the Wookie language of Shyriiwook. You know, from that unlikely little movie that surged: *Star Wars*.)

Brian's buddy Doug served as the lead salesman, and Brian did what he thought he did best: accounting. After a couple of weeks on the road Doug came back with hundreds of business cards from all of the American shoe retailers he had visited, but no orders.

Undeterred, Brian managed to get a last-minute space in a New York footwear show, but the results were more of the same. "In three days, nobody spoke to me. I might as well have been selling car parts, because the buyers didn't get it," Brian said. Brian was trying to sell to everybody, yet nobody got it. Time to paddle harder.

A few weeks of marketing to the masses and it was clear: There was no wave in the retail footwear industry. But he could see the wave forming with a small, specialized customer base, and he knew he had to keep moving in the right direction if he was going to catch it.

The coolest of cool Californian surfers were already heading to Australia on surf trips and bringing three or four pairs of sheepskin boots back for their buddies. The coolest and edgiest of the community—the early adopters—were revealing themselves. That's when the niche became obvious. Brian couldn't sell to the mass market yet, but he *could* sell to the surf market. So he started selling to surf shops exclusively. And the surf shops, albeit slowly, started to buy. Brian had to paddle his hardest at this point, because he was about to jump up on his board and ride that wave.

That first season selling to California surf shops, Brian remembers they sold exactly twenty-eight pairs, which came to a thousand dollars. A weak start for what would become a worldwide fashion brand that today sells over one billion dollars' worth of product annually.

But Brian had confidence—or ignorance, as he puts it—on his side. "To be a successful entrepreneur, you have to have a certain level of ignorance, because if you knew what was ahead when you started out, you'd never start."

Brian was also ignorant of an important marketing problem. Unlike Aussies, Americans associated sheepskin with spun wool, which meant Americans assumed the boots were hot, prickly, and delicate. Far from comfort for your feet. But to Australians, sheepskin is rugged. It breathes. It even wicks moisture, so you can put it on wet feet. That really appeals to surfers, because within ten minutes of putting uggs on, all the moisture is wicked out and your feet are warm, comfortable, and dry. And because sheepskin has natural antimicrobial properties, it doesn't collect bacteria; hence, no odor.

Sheepskin was perfect for footwear; Americans just didn't know it yet. Scratch that—only the über-early adopter Americans who surfed in Australia knew. The rest of America was primed to find out. Even if they weren't aware of it yet, the target customers had a common, fast-growing need, and Brian had the solution.

The next season of sales was far from a barnburner, but that's often how the paddling part intrinsic to this stage goes. The wave is still behind you, and it is hard to measure how big it is. Brian's job during this stage was to paddle hard. He had to get moving on his effort so that he would have enough speed to catch the surging wave building behind him.

The indicators of a surge coming your way? There are typically three. First and foremost, there is extreme loyalty and commitment from the early adopters, either to you or, more often, the concept. In Brian's case it was the use of sheepskin boots. Few American surfers were wearing UGGs at this point; there were only six pairs in circulation a few seasons before, after all. From the very few boots out there, a key surge indicator was visible, albeit barely: The customers using the product were *very* loyal to it. They *only* wore sheepskin boots; there was no alternative. This little bump in the ocean is the energy within the water revealing itself: Customers using your product bring credibility. Customers using your product exclusively bring unquestionable credibility.

Second, those loyal, über-early adopter surfers were encouraging their friends to get a pair, too. And the friends did. For the *surge* watcher, the key indicator is this: Do the early adopters who are loyal to the new product have enough stick-to-it-iveness to fight through social pressure and inertia to convert more early adopters?

The third indicator, as Malcolm Gladwell so eloquently described in *The Tipping Point*, is this: Are the *cool kids* loyal to the new movement? Brands become statements. A newbie surfer who has a crap board, steals waves from the pros, and just sucks at surfing is not one of the "cool kids." If the uncool guy is wearing UGGs, that will actually repulse other surfers from the boots. But if some of the cool kids are sporting the shoe, the initial surge elements are there, and word begins to spread. Word-of-mouth sales mean your offering stands on its own. It's not only delivering on its promise to your customer, it's selling itself. Your product is literally creating its own demand. Time to rally the troops.

The cool people in any surge can't be manufactured, but Brian tried anyway. He hired the most beautiful, sleek-looking models he could find. He put UGGs on their feet and longboards by their sides and ran the ads in *Surfer Magazine*. Beautiful for sure. But cool? Not at all.

Brian told me, "Over beers one day, I explained my trickling sales to one of my surf retailer friends, Robert. He yelled out to the back of his shop, to a couple of local surfer dudes, and said, 'Hey! What do you guys think of UGGs?' And they all said, 'Aww, those UGGs, man, they're so fake! Have you seen those stupid ads? Those models are posers! They can't surf!' I instantly knew I was sending the wrong message to my target market."

People who want to be cooler rally around cooler people. People who want something rally around people who already have that something. Are the "cool kids" of your industry using your thing, or at least something like it? No? Get your thing to the cool kids. Fast.

That's what Brian did. The next season, the skinny models who couldn't tell the difference between a longboard and a cutting board were dumped. FYI—A cutting board is not a surfboard; it's the board on your kitchen counter that you use when you cut up your veggies (or raw meat on Man Day).

Brian grabbed his own camera and took a couple of up-and-coming surfers named Mike Parsons and Ted Robertson out for a photo shoot. Together, Brian, Mike, and Ted hit all the iconic surf walks, and Brian snapped away. Surfers recognized the authenticity in the new ads, lifting UGG from sales of thirty thousand a year out of a van on the beach to over four *hundred* thousand that year. Brian had positioned his business to be in the pocket—the specific spot where the vast majority of your niche marketplace is influenced to make a "go with you" purchase decision.

Brian was ready to build to what he always thought the company could be: a fashion brand. "Everybody thinks I came to California to exploit the surfers, but it was totally by default." Surfers were simply the initial source of energy that started the wave for UGG.

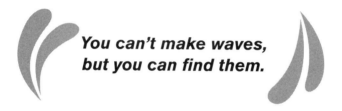

You can't make waves, but you can find them.

Surfers started wearing UGGs to school, and other kids wanted them. Remember? Wannabe cool always emulates already cool. And the moms (cough—wallets—cough, cough) of "wannabes" hit the streets seeking UGGs.

Brian went on to find other ways to expand his market and exposure, eventually creating the phenomenon that made it onto the pages of *People* magazine, the runways at New York Fashion week, and the feet of every cool girl in the great US of A. I'll share more of how he did it in later chapters. For now, I want you to get this one crucial point: You can't make waves, but you can find them.

Yes, that does mean you, too. Your business is not too small for a surge. Your idea is not too narrow for a surge. *You* are not too inexperienced for a surge.

There are no special snowflakes in business. The only difference between you and Brian Smith is, he already rode his wave. This isn't rocket science. If it were, *no way* I'd be doing it. You can do this. You can be the next legend in your industry, and your story begins now.

ACTION STEPS

If you have read my other books, you know I always include action items at the end of each chapter. Why do I do this? Because, if you are like me, you like to read a book through and then go back to it to take action. But, for me, there's one problem with that strategy: I don't go back. Instead, I dig into the next read. Like many people, I discovered I was filling up on great ideas and doing nothing about any of them. But no more. I committed to always taking specific action *while* I am reading a book. And surprise, surprise—I see results.

The same opportunity exists for you. While you could plow ahead and just read (I totally get it, that may work for you), I have found that small but deliberate actions will have an immediate, positive impact on getting your business where you want it.

You will find action items at the end of this chapter and every chapter for which action is required in the remainder of this book. I strongly encourage you to do them, immediately. Most tasks take only a few minutes. Some longer. But if you commit to doing them, you will see results.

To catch a wave, you can't just stand on the beach watching. You actually need to get out there in the ocean and start paddling. Start by doing these tasks now.

ACTION STEPS

1. To see the true opportunity that lies ahead for your business, you must (for now) pull your business out of the equation. Ask yourself, right now—and every day until you find the true answer—"What are my customers doing, regardless of me?"

2. If you think you see a wave, validate it by looking for the cool kids. The nature of being a cool kid is showing off. The early adopters of the Tesla, just like all cool kids, find a way for everyone to know about it. The question is, are they cool? And the answer is quite simple: Cool kids will convince others to do the same; uncool kids won't. Whenever you find potential cool kids, try to find out if they have convinced others to buy. If so, you likely have an imminent wave—a surge.

FINDING YOUR WAVE

REMEMBER THE MOVIE *WORKING GIRL*? I'LL GIVE YOU THE lowdown, just in case you were born after 1975 (gulp). I just politely ask that you don't share with my Man Day compadres that I have *both* seen this movie and can recite lines from it. If they find out I am a closet fan, I would never be invited to a zombie-shoot again.

The movie is about Tess McGill, an executive secretary from Staten Island who is trying to climb the corporate ladder on Wall Street—complete with teased-out hair and an accent straight out of *Real Housewives of New Jersey*. Played by Melanie Griffith, Tess is a real go-getter and she has great ideas, but no one takes her seriously. They think she's "just a secretary," that she couldn't possibly have the smarts or the ingenuity required to put together big deals.

Because she wants to better herself, Tess makes it a habit to research her industry. She reads the industry news. She asks questions. She pays attention and she keeps track. She clips interesting articles for her personal files and jots down ideas.

Early in the movie, she learns that her boss's client wants to invest in the media, but can't seem to get past the restrictions placed on broadcast television ownership. I can still see the scene on the Staten Island Ferry, when she tears an article about a celebrity DJ out of a newspaper and the lightbulb goes on over her head. Radio! It's that eureka moment we all have sometime, we hope many times. It usually starts with, "Hey! What if…?" Don't you love those moments?

Tess ends up posing as her boss and gets in a big ol' mess of trouble, but finally is able to prove her idea was her own thanks to her handy-dandy files. Now, obviously we as entrepreneurs are not Wall Street folks in mergers and acquisitions; far from it. I am bringing up *Working Girl* because Tess's story is an example of an average person finding opportunities simply by paying attention to her industry. (And if you need a pick-me-up when you're feeling less than successful, watch the movie—yeah, it even inspires guys. The last scene will make you think you can do anything. And the last song, "Let the River Run" by Carly Simon, is an entrepreneur's anthem. I dedicated *The Pumpkin Plan* to Ms. Simon, so you know how deep my love goes.)

As you read *Surge*, remember this: You don't have to prove yourself before you can spot the next wave of opportunity for your business. You don't have to be experienced or brilliant; you don't even have to fully understand my wave analogy. Start by paying attention. Watch the horizon. Take note and, when you can, connect the dots. The beginning of your surge could be one random article away—as Tess McGill discovers while freezing her ass off on the Staten Island Ferry, on her way to work.

WAVES IN BUSINESS

As I explained in the first chapter, ocean waves are formed by a confluence of various external forces. Storms, the moon's gravitational pull, earthquakes, landslides, and wind. Science, man. Just science.

Some waves are created in an instant. Take tsunamis, for example. A large piece of land falls into the ocean, or an underground earthquake occurs, and massive amounts of energy are instantly transferred into a wave. It reminds me of the 1970s.

Back in my preteen days, I would lie in my parents' waterbed to watch black and white television. My dad would come out of nowhere and jump on the side of the bed. A massive wave would form instantly and throw me sky-high. (My dad would catch me every so never.) That was an equivalent to a landslide tsunami: completely unsurfable. The physics make it impossible. Surfers know to avoid or ignore the unsurfable waves and concentrate their energy on seeking out long waves.

Short waves have little energy and tend to move slowly. Long waves have the most power and move the fastest. If you have ever been to the beach and observed the long waves that surfers love—the ones that go as far left and as far right as you can see—you know just what kind of power can be contained in one of these waves. The ideal long waves don't break all at once. Instead, they break at a peak part of the wave—the best place to start

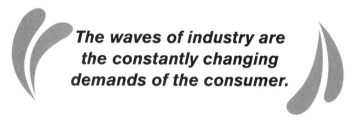

The waves of industry are the constantly changing demands of the consumer.

surfing—and the break continues to peel down the wave as it approaches the beach. A long peeling wave is a wave you can ride hard for a long time. It's the perfect scenario.

Surfers learn to find these best waves not only by watching weather conditions, but also by recognizing the natural patterns and geographic formations that cause great waves to form in the same areas on a regular cycle—very similar to marketplace waves, which are just as surfable.

You don't need a science degree to figure out how to identify the patterns in your industry. Heck, you don't even need to have *passed* science to figure it out. Just as Becky discovered when she started looking for lost money on the street, once you spot the pattern, you'll see it everywhere.

Have you ever thought about the number of industries and businesses out there? From crushing cardboard to creating computers, there's an industry for everything. The size of the ocean of business is practically unimaginable. And every square inch of it is shifting with countless changes. Countless waves.

The waves of industry are the constantly changing demands of the consumer. This is more commonly referred to as *market momentum*. A different name, but a wave by any other name is still a wave. And the properties are the same.

Market momentum (a wave) is formed by trends (wind), or sometimes a massive market disruption (earthquake). Tsunamis of industry happen, but they aren't rideable. The physics of market tsunamis prohibit it. No one company rode the mobile technology wave, though all of them purport to have done it. The tsunami represents a massive shift in consumer behavior, resulting in countless distinct surges. So while it is nice to pound your chest and say you are riding the mobile technology tsunami, you're not. It's like saying you are riding the wave of business and commerce. Yeah, we all are, but that's not a wave. It's the ocean. You're riding a specific, cresting wave—perhaps a massive one—that has triggered a segment of customers to start moving in a certain direction. It's a trend wave.

TREND WAVES

Trend waves are very rideable. The tsunami of mobile technology is so broad and so massive that no single company is riding it. But the waves it has triggered, like smartphones (Samsung and Apple are "hanging ten" on that wave), smartphone cases (Speck has carved up that one), the blending of smartphone and on-demand transportation services (Uber and Lyft are all over that), mobile fitness (just look at Fitbit), mobile app development (being surfed by the mostly bearded team at Fueled.com), and many more, are being surfed by company after company. And many of them, like Uber and Speck, "came out of nowhere." They didn't, really, but like UGG, they were just paddling hard in front of the wave to get in perfect sync with it. Those companies were putting their efforts into timing the trend wave when everybody else was standing on the beach.

SURFABLE WAVES

Surfable waves are those formed by the shifting demands of the customer. The shifts in customer demand can be big or small; subtle or in-your-face; slow, long, or "Holy crap, where the hell did that come from? Hey wait a second; is that already gone? Thank God!" meteoric. Collectively, all these different forms of shifting customer demand are simply trends.

Trends will move fastest when they move toward an underserved hole in the market, much as wind moves toward low pressure in the atmosphere. The longer a trend continues to move, the bigger the market momentum wave it forms. The wave, in turn, goes on absorbing power from the trend; and if it continues unopposed by other competing trends or industries over a long enough time, it will grow to be really large. If you can see the patterns at work in your specific niche, as great surfers do, you can begin to predict where and when these waves will begin to form.

I'm such a geek for this stuff, but I realize not everyone wants to dig deep into the correlation between surfing and trends in business. If all of this science talk is making your eyes glaze over, here's a real-world example that changed all of our lives. Social media momentum was started by the relentless thirst we humans have to communicate, share, and show pictures of every single damned piece of food we eat (the wave). The personal computer became accessible to everyday folks by the early 1980s, and by the middle of that decade modems had gained popularity. All the elements for a new form of communication and sharing were in place. The wind of customer demand started to shift. A wave of bulletin board systems (BBS) formed, allowing people to post messages and comment on posts by others. People could now engage in deep conversations without ever leaving their houses. "Wow! That grainy picture of porridge looks a lot like grainy porridge."

By 1994, the peak of BBS use, the BBS wave included about seventeen million users through Internet connection players like AOL, Compuserve, and Prodigy.

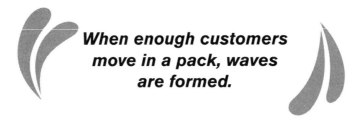

When enough customers move in a pack, waves are formed.

Then the Mosaic web browser made it "easy" to surf the web and create your own site via HTML. The BBS wave crashed onto the beach. Forums, site-specific FAQs, live chat, and search killed BBS. With overwhelming amounts of new data being generated every day, major search engines came about to make sense of it all.

Companies like Yahoo! and then Google rode the crap out of these waves. Then the social media tide began to rise, spawning countless different waves ridden by the likes of WordPress, Twitter, LinkedIn, and thousands of non-household name brands that have done extremely well for themselves. Some got up on their board only momentarily and wiped out (MySpace); others ride like pros (Facebook—for now, at least). Customer demand is always shifting, and new waves are always being formed, ready to be surfed… by you.

The lesson is this: The customer is always moving. Always. When enough customers move in a pack, waves are formed. When the wave forms, it can grow or stay small. You just need to spot the wave and determine if it is the ideal size for you to ride. (Don't worry, I will teach you how to do both in this book). Then, if it's a good wave for you, you need to start paddling in front of it with the hope—not the guarantee—that you will catch the surge and have the ride of a lifetime.

Will waves eventually crash onto the rocks? Yes! All waves crash onto the rocks, or fizzle out as they roll onto the beach. When you ride a wave, it will crash against the shore at some point. I guarantee it. The key is to ride it as hard as you can for as long as you can, but constantly keep watching for the wave to wash out. As Seth Godin explains in his must-read book, *Purple Cow*: While your consumer base buys your remarkable offering, you need to milk it for all it's worth, because it isn't going to last.

Most of those companies that noticed the social media wave coming early on, and found a way to harness that wave, tapped into a massive energy that still pushes them along. The smart companies are riding that wave like mad, carving it up every way they can think of. Yet their leaders know they need to be ready to get off the wave as it peters out or collapses in on itself.

It is a strange, somewhat contradictory, coexistence. Ride a wave for all it's worth, while simultaneously preparing to get off the second you see it approaching the rocks. And the farther you ride an existing wave, the farther you'll need to paddle back out to get in front of the next. As a result, it is really hard to ride great wave after great wave. But it can be done. Remember when IBM made computers? Beyond making computers, they paddled out in front of the personal computer wave and dominated it. Then they spotted the end of their wave and smartly jumped off. They sold the computer division to a Chinese company, Lenovo, and paddled out in front of the consulting wave. Now they are surfing a killer wave yet again.

Don't confuse riding consecutive waves, as IBM and others have done, with riding simultaneous waves. No one can do that. Now, before you get your undies in a bunch and ramble on about master surfers Elon Musk or Richard Branson, or any other entrepreneur who is running a handful, or dozens, or hundreds of companies at once—they're not. They surely have an uncanny ability to spot waves and can place their corporate board in the perfect spot, but they inevitably get someone else to do the paddling and surfing. They plug in the perfect number two to lead the companies.

You want to ride the wave that is clearly already upon you and *that you are in front of*— not one you need to chase.

Maybe you have uncanny wave-spotting abilities too. But it's unlikely. Predicting far-off trends is really hard. As Rahit Bhargava shares in his book, *Non-Obvious*, the easiest trends to spot are the imminent ones, not future possibilities. Most entrepreneurs are best served by concentrating on spotting the imminent, niche market wave and focusing all of their own energy on paddling in front of it to the perfect spot. You want to ride the wave that is clearly already upon you *and* that you are in front of—not one you need to chase.

CAPTURING AN INDUSTRY SHIFT

Just like the ocean, individual markets and even whole industries are constantly shifting. Nothing in the world ever stays the same, and business is no different. Markets grow or shrink; they rarely stay at a constant level. Consumer demand grows and shrinks: Whole industry categories change in structure, grow, or disappear altogether. Remember VCRs? Anyone? Bueller? Bueller?

Have you dumped your DVD player for a Blu-Ray device? Or do you simply stream all of your movies and TV shows from Amazon or Netflix? If you missed the streaming wave, don't fret; the next wave is right behind it. Home entertainment is just one example. Look in *your* target industry and you'll undoubtedly find similar shifts. The examples are endless.

These changes come in all sizes. Some changes are tsunami-sized and bring sudden, massive disruption, as I explained to you earlier. Others are tidal shifts. The VCR was an individual wave that let people watch movies at home. Home entertainment, on the other hand, is a tidal shift. It encompasses all kinds of home entertainment, from online streaming to shopping from the couch to a kick-butt sound system that shakes your soul. (Sometimes literally: Check out how TheButtKicker.com is riding this wave.)

Again, tidal shifts are too large for *any* company—I am talking to you, Google—to find all their unique advantages. Tidal shifts tend to lift or change the direction of everyone in the ocean, not simply change the landscape for one industry or market. Don't try to catch a tidal shift. You can't. Instead, master an individual wave or trend *within* the tidal shift that affects your customers.

Waves may not be as big and powerful as tidal shifts or tsunamis, but they can provide just the momentum *your* business needs to shoot to the top and achieve incredible success. Some waves are small enough to be manageable for any size company. And while tidal shifts are very few in number, individual waves are everywhere. In fact, with so many waves available, the odds are good that you'll find one no one else is riding, leaving you plenty of room to work your wave to your company's best advantage.

So how do you find the wave that's right for you? Well, before you paddle out into the surf, it's important to do a little wave-watching. Surfers learn to read several factors to predict where and when they are going to find that perfect wave. You need to do the same.

First, analyze the part of the ocean in which you are going to surf. Everything, from weather conditions to geography and tides, figures into the equation. I explain this extensively in *The Pumpkin Plan*. I use a (notably, very sexy) colossal-pumpkin farming analogy in that book, but all of the strategies connect and work together. The best part, and arguably the only part of the ocean you can surf in successfully, is where your company's *unique* offering caters to a *specific* type of top client in a *repeatable* and *consistent* fashion.

Look at the history of your top clients. History is a good indicator of things to come. Call them cycles, trends, or fads, the bottom line is this: Whatever's old becomes new again. To find where your waves will form, you first need to be a historian of your industry. What happened before is very likely to happen again, just in a new flavor. Organic fruits and vegetables were once all that existed. Then they were replaced by corporate-grown produce ripened using cheaper methods. And now the organics are back. History repeats.

Mom used to stay home and raise the kids, but then the wave of dual-income families took over, and now *that* wave is crashing as more and more families have one parent at home raising the kids. History repeats. Often with a slightly different spin. Shout out to all the Mr. Moms.

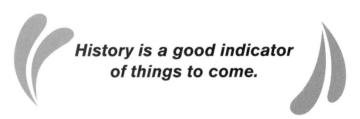

History is a good indicator of things to come.

Shorts used to be super long (just look at those old-fashioned beach photos); then they went super short (Google pictures of Bruce Jenner... when he was Bruce Jenner), then long again (remember Jams?), and now they are getting shorter and shorter again. I suspect that by the end of this decade we will be back to the constant risk of seeing something we really, really don't want to see—thanks to short shorts. To confirm this wave (and I really don't want to), just see if the cool kids are wearing them.

Sunglasses are big, then small, then big, then small. Cars are the same. Circus freak shows have given way to the circus of "reality TV" freaks. History just *repeats*. In fact, as you read this book, I myself am trying to surf the wave of resurgent history—self-publishing.

Poor Richard's Almanack, Benjamin Franklin's annual mid-1700s almanac which immediately became a perennial bestseller in the American colonies, was... wait for it... wait for it—self-published. Granted, Ben was a printer by trade. But self-publishing was the way to go for a long, long period of time. I think it is fair to assume that the original Ten Commandments, carved on two slabs of stone, were not edited, printed, and published by Random House. Those stones were self-chiseled. Okay, technically they were "inscribed by the finger of God." Po-ta-to, po-tah-to.

Then a new wave full of publishing houses came, and self-publishing basically vanished. But, as history repeats itself, self-publishing started to form into a wave again. By 2008, more books were self-published than marketed by traditional publishers. The quality of self-publishing started to rival—ahem, even *surpass*—that of the publishing houses. I saw the relentless energy in the wave, and parted ways with my traditional publisher to self-publish my last book, *Profit First*. And this one.

Speaking of "traditional," that is another indicator of a new wave. When an industry has something traditional about it, the word "traditional" should be replaced with "crashing." Traditional music is always dying out while, simultaneously, new music forms. This "new" music will, of course, become traditional over time, which then means *that* music has started its crash into the rocks, and yet *newer* music—perhaps a new spin on the old—will replace it.

Traditional publishing is being replaced with self-publishing, on-demand publishing, electronic publishing, and the newest wave that I am trying to paddle in front of: interactive publishing, in which you don't read just words, but also watch video, listen to audio, converse (in instant video chats between me and you), and so much more. Smell-o-book? Why the heck not? You know you want the scent of my mom's famous pumpkin bread baking in the oven to fill the room as you read my next book. (As a total but relevant aside, I am working on a book entitled *Hardwired*, for future release, which explains consumers' natural, hardwired "buy" triggers. Four years ago I conducted an experiment with mom's homemade pumpkin bread, and sure enough, even the most educated, knowledgeable experts responded predictably. I found that there is, in fact, a crystal ball for individual human behavior. And to some degree there is a crystal ball for a surge. It's called "tradition.")

The "traditional" approach is always poised to go bye-bye, and a new wave with a new approach is always waiting to form. Banks were "traditionally" only open from ten a.m. to four p.m., Monday through Friday. That's how we got the term "bankers hours." Then some banks noticed that people who had money to deposit may actually be *working* to make that money, so they started to stay open later one night a week, then added limited hours on Saturdays and even on Sundays. Then, to make themselves even more convenient, bank branches started popping up in strip malls and inside grocery stores. But now, with the tidal shift of debit and credit cards, direct deposit, ATMs, and the Internet, people can have 24/7 access to their money without ever going *in* a bank. Because of this, the banks trying to get ahead of the wave are closing branches—and the banks that understand the power of SURGE exist *only* online and have no branches at all.

Another way to spot a swell forming in the marketplace is to watch for consumers trying to figure out their own workarounds for "traditional" solutions. When customers want something and no one is offering it, they will seek their own solutions rather than grin and bear it. They will form the beginning ripples of a new wave.

If you think about it, you've already spotted incoming waves in your industry or others. You've noticed when fashions come back in style, when systems become obsolete. You know what used to be the norm in your business, or in your region, and why that changed. You just haven't yet analyzed it from this perspective.

I graduated from Virginia Tech. In the middle of campus is a massive field that students walk across to get from their dorms to classes. Countless times a day, students walk back and forth across this field. The university installed paved sidewalks crossing the field, and yet the students have beaten down their own paths, those that will take them most directly to their classes (and beyond to the bars). The sidewalks are barely used by the students seeking the shortest walks to their classes. If Virginia Tech had paid attention to the dirt paths worn by students, they would have seen that the students provided them with the answer to where to place the sidewalks. *The solution was presented by the customers themselves.* Observe your clients. Watch the paths they blaze. Then go pave the paths for them.

Another great place to watch for waves is in foreign markets. You'll see that waves *over there* often become waves *over here*. The wave of sheepskin boots in Australia was a huge indicator that there could be a wave for sheepskin boots in the US, and as you know, our friend Brian Smith rode that massive wave to billions in revenue. Phil Romano did the same with Romano's Macaroni Grill. He went to Italy, saw the custom of having fresh-cut flowers and open jugs of wine at every table in small Italian bistros, and offered the same at his Texas restaurant. He surfed that wave of casual dining—where you simply told the waiter how many glasses of wine you had as you sniffed the flowers—and opened over two hundred locations throughout North America, Europe, and the Middle East.

The Internet exploded in the US, and then it exploded throughout the world. The wildly successful TV show, *The Office*, was first a wild success in the UK after it launched in 2001. *The Office* then rolled into the US, launching in 2005 to long-running success here. *Shark Tank* in the US was *Dragon's Den* in the UK first. In fact, many successful US shows started in Britain. And the trend will move on. What's hot in New York City today will be the hot thing next year in Tokyo. The hip thing in Copenhagen will hit the streets soon in Johannesburg. What is trending *there* will likely trend *here*. Just pray that the trend in men's short shorts doesn't spread. No pun intended, sicko.

I shared a lot of different examples in this section because I wanted you to see that spotting trends is not complicated. Sure, there are many ways to go about it, and it can be a challenge at first to figure out if a wave is worth riding—and if the timing is right. That said, once you get the hang of it, you'll spot opportunities left and right. Simply form a habit of constant observation, and the patterns will reveal themselves, just as Becky Blanton has found and continues to find money every day in "catch and hold" spots.

LANDSLIDES AND IMMINENT WAVES

And while you're watching for waves, don't forget to also watch for landslides, because they can cause many waves, including some friggin' *huge* waves. When massive incumbent companies make innovations that require their vendors, competitors, and even un-suspecting "victims" to change, these business landslides can cause a series of residual waves to form: Amazon releases the Kindle, cre-ating an e-reader landslide. Competing products like Nook and Kobo and even the iPad come into play. New self-publishing ser-vices like Smashwords and DocStoc explode into life. Savvy tra-ditional publishers change their model. Sure, the wave in e-read-ers began before Amazon, but the point isn't so much who started it; the point is that one massive player eventually made a gigantic splash that added a lot of energy to the wave.

If you take a drive on the nearest interstate highway, you will notice a trend: more trucks. More and more eighteen-wheelers are cruising the highway, and more and more are coming. Why? Because of Walmart and Amazon, along with many others. The explosion of home delivery has changed the transportation and logistics market forever. The wave started back in the late 1990s and has gotten massive amounts of energy because of the big players in Internet commerce. The opportunities? Everything from wheel manufacturers (e.g., more efficient, wider truck wheels) to software companies (improved logistics software) could find waves to ride here. Construction of distribution centers along highways for e-commerce businesses. The invention of the TrailerTail, the aerodynamic metal "tail" you might have noticed on the back of eighteen-wheelers, which improves fuel efficiency. The number of waves is almost incalculable. The number of opportunities that await you is *immense*. And the next massive logistics wave is already out there on the horizon: drones and autonomous vehicles.

Of course there are victims of landslides, too. When McDonald's decided to offer a salad with cranberries, the entire cranberry market shifted. At least temporarily, prices soared and small companies like Jimmy's Cookies in Fairlawn, New Jersey, for example, which needed cranberries to make cookies, had to scramble to find a new spot to ride on the wave that didn't require cranberries. The solid leadership at Jimmy's Cookies continued to watch the pocket of the wave the company was riding and made a quick carve to navigate the fast break in the wave.

But there is an even more dangerous scenario out there in the ocean: paddling too soon. Yes, drone home delivery is coming and self-driving cars are on their way, but they are not imminent (at least, as of when I published this book). You can create a business today that will capture the energy of the self-driving car wave, but your business will be paddling a long time and is likely to run out of juice before the marketplace is a reality. If you want to be a surge pro, always, and I mean always, look for imminent waves and ensure that you are positioned in front of them.

HOW I FOUND MY OWN WAVE

As I mentioned to you in the introduction, I am different from a traditional author in that I don't write books… at least, not at first. Before I even consider what I want to write about, I take these concepts and apply them to my own businesses, and/or start a new one to test them out. I am currently an owner in three companies, all guinea pigs: a membership organization, a manufacturer, and a tech startup. I did all the stuff I put in *The Toilet Paper Entrepreneur* before I wrote about it. I followed the niche specialization strategy I documented in *The Pumpkin Plan* to grow my data-forensics firm and sold that company to a Fortune 500 before I wrote the book. And I have done the same with *Surge*. I did this stuff for myself before I wrote this "manual" on how you can do it. Here are the results I have experienced from *Surge* (so far):

My experience began with my third book, *Profit First*, which of course you have read three or four times by now (hint, hint). In case you haven't read it—now *my* undies are in a bunch—I would summarize it as a new way for entrepreneurs to make their businesses wildly more profitable by following a profoundly simple method: Take your profit first, always. It is the "pay yourself" principle applied to business.

After writing *Profit First*, I started to hear from readers who wanted to find accountants and bookkeepers who could work with the *Profit First* system. You see, until now the traditional (holy cannoli, there's that word again!) system of making your business profitable was to follow the traditional (yikes!) formula of: Sales - Expenses = Profit.

But, as you may be acutely aware yourself, most companies aren't profitable. They survive check to check. So in *Profit First* I teach a new approach: Sales - Profit = Expenses. In other words, I took the "pay yourself first principle" and applied it to my business. This subtle shift has had massive impact. Businesses implementing and adhering to this process experienced immediate improvements and skyrocketing profitability. But there was one problem (ah, another indicator of a potential wave). Many companies couldn't get their existing accountant and bookkeeper to show interest in, let alone support, the *Profit First* concept. And without accounting professionals' support, entrepreneurs struggled with the adhering part.

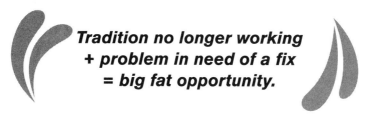

Tradition no longer working + problem in need of a fix = big fat opportunity.

These entrepreneurs wanted their businesses to be more profitable and begged their existing accountants and bookkeepers to actively guide, support, and hold them accountable to the *Profit First* process. Yet their traditional accountants and bookkeepers said no!

Tradition no longer working + problem in need of a fix = big fat opportunity. Like Tess McGill, I was having my own, guy's version of the *Working Girl* eureka moment. I could see that an imminent wave was upon the accounting and bookkeeping industry, a wave I could ride to propel a new service offering. Surely there were some progressive accountants and bookkeepers who wanted to serve their clients in the new way the clients wanted to be served? If I could find them, I could create an offering that empowered this new wave of accounting professionals to serve the new wave of entrepreneurs seeking far more consultative accounting professionals.

To help find that perfect wave, I did some research on the current state of the market. I started to observe bookkeepers and accountants to find out what the "coolest" ones were saying and, more importantly, doing. They were transitioning from data entry masters to advising their clients on fiscal health. They saw that software like Xero, Sage, Wave, QuickBooks, and Freshbooks were becoming so technically sophisticated that the software compiled the traditional bookkeeping and tax returns automatically. They saw that big players were (and still are) trying to gobble up the easy—albeit dying—clerical work. Enter firms like H&R Block and Jackson Hewitt. The independent accountants and bookkeepers who were trying to do the same thing in the same way they always had were responding by trying to compete on price and getting crushed in the middle as a result.

The waves of traditional accounting and bookkeeping are crashing hard. But the "cool kid" (early adopter) accountants and bookkeepers showed me where the new wave was rising. So I created a new business model to ride this wave. Using the popular features from my book *Profit First*, I developed a comprehensive system that helps independent bookkeepers and accountants move away from the dying transactional services they used to perform and into an advisory model where they can thrive. My firm's promise is quite simple: Join Profit First Professionals and move from a commodity-based, transactional accounting business to a done-for-you, consultative, high-margin, high-value profit advisor model.

By aligning the swelling needs of our business clients—independent bookkeepers and accountants—to the unique abilities and services that we offer via Profit First Professionals, we have caught this wave and are doing everything within our power to ride it hard and fast.

You know that feeling when you spot an opportunity in your industry, one that no one else seems to see? What a rush, right? Even if you haven't acted on all of your ideas—or even one of them—I know you've experienced the excitement of honing in on something that, once you spot it, seems so obvious and promising. Heck, you may have launched your business on an idea born of spotting an untapped opportunity in the marketplace. Do you get what I'm trying to tell you? You've already done this, at least once. You *have.* The only difference is that you will now be more deliberate about the process, gaining confidence, and leveraging what you see. And this book will give you the tools to see it all the way through.

WHERE WILL YOU FIND YOUR WAVE?

Where are these waves forming in your market? Begin looking at your target market now. Look at the history of the niche—where it has been through cycles in the past and where those cycles could lead it in the future. Thanks to the Internet, this is an easy step. Just do a search for "history of _____" and insert the niche or industry you are targeting.

As a second step, seek out the target market's experts. Find out what they are saying about the trends of the industry. Unlike experts who try to predict the future and seem to get it wrong way more often than they get it right, look for feedback on the new things that are *already starting to happen.* If no one is wearing short shorts, they may yet become a new trend; but for you to start making a junk-hiding-cover or sunglasses that are shaded so dark you are effectively blind would be way premature. Look for what the experts say is starting to happen and validate it. Look for a wave forming from a dying "tradition." And surely look for waves *over there* that are repeating *over here.*

Just as surfers do, look at waves that are imminently upon you. Surfers don't care about the waves that are miles out in the ocean. They don't care about those that are even a hundred yards out. Not at all. Surfers are measuring the next few waves. If the next wave stinks, they let it pass as they sum up the one immediately behind it.

The marketplace is constantly rolling out waves. Don't try to predict what is going to happen five or ten years from now. Those waves are miles out in the ocean. They are impossible to spot, and even if by some miracle you did spot one, they aren't close enough to shore to surf. Just look for the waves that are already formed and approaching with growing size and speed. Then, once you've seen where these new waves are, take a look at how you might align what your company offers with what your customers will need to take advantage of an oncoming wave.

Once you've identified that wave, you'll need to begin paddling with everything you've got to get in front of it. You want to put yourself in position to capture that wave, and have it carry your business forward. This is the true power of waves, the power that you must capture.

A niche is the community of customers who make up a wave. That individual wave is the movement of that niche… the new direction they are taking and you are riding. First, identify your niche (the specific and targeted group of consumers you are serving), and then identify the wave (the specific movement that niche is making).

This energy is propelling Profit First Professionals far more than anything Ron Saharyan, who is the cofounder and managing director of our company, or I could have created on our own. The power behind it is not marketing, advertising, or social media. That's just paddling. Profit First Professionals has a powerful momentum because the industry itself is changing, and this change has created a wave that we've managed to catch and hope we have the skill to keep surfing. We couldn't have created this type of wave on our own, but we can ride this wave to propel our business forward.

You're positioned to do the same, quite possibly even better. How do I know? Because every business and every industry has a new wave forming. And that new wave is always forming now. As in *right now*.

So take one more look at all the beautiful waves out there in the ocean. Take one last sip of coconut water, grab your board, and run out there into the ocean. You are about to become a surfing pro. You are about to harness the *surge*.

ACTION STEPS

1. Tradition is a lead indicator of something that is going away and yielding to something new. See through the traditions for the new wave right behind them. Ask your current top clients:

    a. What is traditional about their industry?

    b. What do they traditionally do in their business?

    c. Who are the traditional players?

    d. What traditions are changing or going away?

2. Hop on the Internet and do a quick search for "history of _____" and put in the niche you are focusing on. Then do another search for "trends in the _____ industry (or markct)" and put your niche in the blank space. Between these two searches, you should sight a plethora of waves.

3. Check out the industry experts. Read their books, see them speak, watch their videos, or use my favorite strategy and interview them for an article or blog post you write. Get their input on:

    a. What is happening in the industry right now?

    b. How it has changed over the past few years?

    c. How do they see things playing out over the next twelve months?

SEPARATE

Let's pick on Walmart for a minute. (It's easy to poke a gorilla when you are safely tucked away behind the pages of a book… in oversized, ratty sweatpants.) Walmart is massive. They have mastered the marketplace for the "need it *now* at the absolute best price" crowd. But even with all of that power, Walmart still doesn't come to mind first as an online retailer, even though they have been trying to make inroads on the web for a long time. Which online retailer is the go-to for finding great deals? Amazon. You didn't need me to tell you that; you probably have a box from Amazon sitting on your porch right now.

Amazon brings in roughly one-eighth of Walmart's sales volume. Even though Walmart crushes Amazon in overall revenue, Walmart's online sales only account for about two to three percent of their overall sales, which ranks them somewhere around one-sixth of Amazon's online revenue. Walmart may own the local retail space, but in cyberspace, they're still an also-ran.

No matter how big your company, the lesson is pretty obvious: Even the established "kings of the beach" can't surf more than one wave. Do you remember the nickname my mastermind Man Day buddies gave me? "Bob." You know why they called me "Bob?" Because I was the surfer who paddled in circles, *bobbing* in the ocean all day. I wasn't the only Bob, though. The ocean is full of Bobs. Most Bobs are busy chasing every little ripple, always looking for a better wave, but then as one starts to lift them up, they use it to look for a yet better wave. Bobs never seek out a single wave to surf. They just bob on all of them and never ride. If we're lucky, at a certain point all Bobs realize that our nickname is really spelled with *two* o's.

My Bob days were over once I shifted my focus to the natural direction in which my niche was moving. I then figured out how to build on the proven business growth strategies I developed earlier in my entrepreneurial adventure and, because it is my way, I came up with a system. (Systems are my jam. Nothing is more satisfying than a good system.) SURGE isn't just a goal, or the promise of this book. SURGE is also a handy-dandy acronym I came up with to help you remember this process.

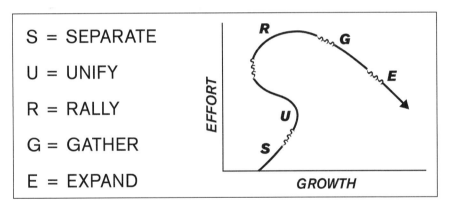

I find it's easier to remember systems when they are paired with a graphic, so here's one I created that you may find helpful. (You don't want to see my first drawing of this graph. Let's just say I did not miss my calling as a visual artist!) I created this graph to demonstrate how much your effort and rate of growth will shift during each stage of SURGE.

Looking at the graph, you'll see that the vertical axis shows the effort, and the horizontal axis shows the growth. The S stage (Separate) requires low but rapidly increasing effort and results in quick initial growth. Once you separate out your target market, you know who to sell to and who *not* to sell to, which makes it easier for you to determine *how* to sell. If you simply make a committed decision to target a niche, it is comparatively easy to experience quick initial growth with little effort—a nice reward for decisiveness.

The U stage (Unify) often requires additional effort, and your business may seem to plateau or experience reverse growth for a short time. This is because you are researching in this stage, searching for patterns, for what your niche needs now and what it and other niches may need in the future. Because you are focused on finding and serving these needs, some of the customers in your original niche will not be served by you and may leave. It takes guts to make it through this stage, but unifying is the only way to get to the R, G, and E stages.

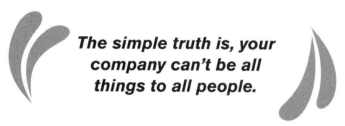

The simple truth is, your company can't be all things to all people.

The R stage (Rally) requires you to continue to increase your effort as you empower your community to rally around your mission. You'll need to train them to effectively spread the word, to help your staff and customers make your Rally Cry part of who they are. Once this process takes hold, your required effort will decrease and yet your growth will begin a fast climb. This is that delicate phase when you stop paddling and start riding.

The G stage (Gather) is when your marketplace does the heavy lifting for you, automatically. The marketing effort required from you is now in steady decline, while your business growth is steadily increasing.

In the E stage (Expand), the trend of less effort and faster growth continues, as you are now repeating the core growth process you have mastered in prior markets with new targeted markets.

In this chapter, we'll cover the S in SURGE: Separate. The simple truth is, your company can't be all things to all people. Stop being unfocused. Stop hoping for the perfect wave to come right to you at the perfect angle. And for God's sake, stop standing on the beach pointing at the other surfers. The marketplace has thousands of waves, so pick up your board and take inventory of your resources. If you concentrate all your efforts on a single wave, serving a single niche, you will be able to ride like a pro with nary a thought of the eight hundred-pound gorilla surfing the wave in front of you. Except maybe to say, "WTF? Who taught that gorilla to surf? And what is up with his nasty-looking sweatpants?"

WHERE REVENUE MEETS SMILEY FACES

Mom lied. You shouldn't treat everyone the same. I learned the hard way that if want to ride the wave all the way to industry domination, I actually need to do the opposite. I need to stop treating everyone the same. Give my best to my best clients and not to the rest. Then, clone my best customers. It is my best clients who will ultimately reveal my niche, or my single wave. Then, dump the bad clients, or better yet, let my competitor deal with them. Thanks, Ma.

If you are operating a young company, or a company struggling to stay afloat, you may think this is crazy talk. Dump clients, Mike? Why would anyone with even half a brain do that? It's simple: If you devote your energy to clients who are barely profitable and use up a disproportionate amount of your time and energy, you are wasting your scant resources on clients who will weigh you down and keep you stuck on the shore.

If you read my book, *The Pumpkin Plan*, what I'm about to share with you will be familiar. Even if you're tempted to skip this chapter, I'm hoping you'll read on, because the urge to welcome any and all clients is strong, my friend. It's easy to get sucked back into serving anyone and everyone… or maybe just this *one* client who doesn't quite fit your top client mold. Or two. Four, tops. We all need a refresher from time to time—even little old me.

As I detailed in *The Pumpkin Plan,* massively profitable businesses cater to their top clients, build their focus on the unique needs of those clients, and systematize the whole enchilada. This is also how giant pumpkins grow to be newsworthy prize-winners: pumpkin farmers assess which pumpkins in their patch are the healthiest and remove all the other pumpkins from the vine so that all of the water, sunlight, fertilizer, and love goes to the most promising pumpkins. If you want to ride the SURGE you need to ride it in a niche where you are catering to your *greatest* clients and their clones.

If your business is doing something between hundreds of thousands and hundreds of millions of dollars in revenue, you are already in the position to find your niche by studying your customer list. Start with picking your favorites from that list and then clone them by following the next steps in SURGE. (If you're just starting out and don't have the dollars or the customers yet, you'll find SURGE preparation suggestions at the end of each of the next few chapters.)

If you want to ride the SURGE you need to ride it in a niche where you are catering to your greatest clients and their clones.

Who are your favorites, the top ten percent of your customers? Your rock star clients are usually those who are fun to do business with and pay you well. And who are your "cringe-worthy" customers? These are the customers who, when their numbers pop up on Caller ID, you quickly put through to voicemail. They are usually regulars on your collections list and give you grief for every little thing. If you want to see how your fave clients and your cringe clients are affecting your bottom line, run a profit analysis comparing the two sets. If you don't know how to conduct a per-client profit analysis, use a qualified accountant or bookkeeper. Cough—go to ProfitFirstProfessionals.com—cough—shameless plug—cough.

In *The Pumpkin Plan*, I share a detailed "client assessment" strategy that guides you through the sorting of clients. The client assessment worksheet is available for free download at my website, www.MikeMichalowicz.com, in the Resources section. No, it's nothing like the sorting hat in *Harry Potter*, although that would be way more fun. Here is the ultra-simplified version:

Step One: Sort your clients by revenue per client over the past twelve months.

Step Two: Organize your list so that the clients who bring in the most revenue are at the top. These are the clients who love you best. Know how I know? They keep buying stuff from you. Always remember this: *Customers speak the truth through their wallets, not their words.* I suggest highlighting that one on your Kindle, writing it in your notes and tattooing it to your spouse's forehead so you are reminded every morning when you wake up. Always measure your clients' engagement in your offering by their spend, not their spit (words).

Step Three: Look at each customer on your list and put a smiley face next to your rock star clients. These are the customers *you* love best. Then, add a frowny face next to your cringe-worthy clients. (What? Frowny is *so* a word.)

Step Four: Cross out the lowest ten percent of customers, the ones who bring in the least amount of revenue and earned a frowny face. These are your worst clients and they must be destroyed. Okay, not really destroyed per se. But they're definitely getting cut.

Step Five: Circle the highest ten percent of customers, those who bring in the most revenue and also earned smiley faces. These are your best customers, the clients you want to clone, the clients who will reveal to you *everything* you need to know about your niche.

KNOWING YOUR CLIENTS BETTER THAN THEY KNOW THEMSELVES

It is at the intersection of customers-who-love-you and customers-you-love where the magic happens. This is where you find your niche, the wave that will take your business to the next level. The answer is in what your best and favorite customers have in common and what they need the most.

Now that you have your best-est clients circled, document what you know about each customer. What industry or community is she in? If you run a donut shop, this might not seem to matter, but it does, so give it your best shot. Is the client male or female? How old? What's the size of his business?

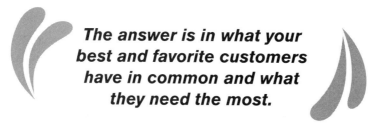

The answer is in what your best and favorite customers have in common and what they need the most.

Look for similarities in the information you documented about your clients. Are they in similar industries or communities? Are they demographically the same? Psychographically? Sometimes you will find that there are many similarities among your best clients, and sometimes you won't find many. But at this stage you should have a manageable list of potential niches, even if your top clients are all distinct. You will have fewer niches if there is some overlap in your top customers. You will have one niche for all your top clients if you have already mastered this vertical.

This Separate phase is so critical because you have to choose where you are going to spend your limited energy, time, and money to try to catch the larger momentum of your marketplace wave. Without doing this separation to show you where to look for that wave, you could be looking forever without really knowing what you're looking for.

As you already know, I use myself as a guinea pig before I share a concept in one of my books. When I launched Profit First Professionals (PFP), I implemented the Separate phase the second we passed the quarter-million dollar revenue mark. A lot of research and a few key questions to the clients we wanted to clone (I share those questions in *The Pumpkin Plan*), and we had a clear avatar of an Olympic-level prospect for our business. I knew the ideal-size business, the goals and aspirations, the history and struggles, the demographics, the psychographics, everything about my ideal client.

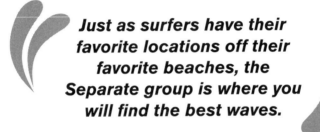

> **Just as surfers have their favorite locations off their favorite beaches, the Separate group is where you will find the best waves.**

Why am I not sharing the numbers? Why am I not giving you *all* the details about a perfect PFP client? Because I am running the business today and trying to surf this massive marketplace wave as far as I can. I don't want to give the other surfers in the ocean (who may decide to read this book) the SURGE recipe for my marketplace wave. As you start riding a surge, you shouldn't share all the details either. Keep your secret surfing cove secret.

I will, however, give you the details for another company I built and sold. My first company installed computer networks. I was a "Bob" in that business for *years*. On the verge of adding the second "o" to my name, I started to realize how exhausting and fruitless it was to serve anybody who owned a small business, and I picked a wave. That wave was hedge fund brokers, and I would supply their Information Technology (IT) needs. I picked this wave by following the exact strategy I outlined above: Sort the customers, pick the best, and clone them.

IT services for hedge fund brokers became my niche. I knew the exact avatar:

1. A hedge fund that managed between a hundred million and a billion in assets. The larger guys had their own people in-house; the smaller guys couldn't afford me.
2. The managing partner was still involved in picking the IT company, but the company was growing fast enough that he was unlikely to be involved much.
3. The managing partner was a male, aged thirty-five to fifty, and thought technology was cool. He also thought that the only thing cooler than technology was himself. Yeah, my best clients had a "little" touch of ego, for sure. And just as they demanded to have the newest Ferrari in the parking lot, they demanded that the newest technology be parked in their office.
4. The company had to be located in the Northeastern US, though once I was up and surfing the wave, this expanded nationally, then globally.

There are more details, but you can see how specific I was. With this clarity, it was *super* easy to see the marketplace and measure the dynamics of the wave. It was crystal clear where I needed to surf.

When *you* give the same—or greater—specificity to your marketplace, you will likely have the same experience I did. First you will notice that before, when you were a "Bob," there was competition everywhere. Now there is hardly *any* competition. Maybe even none. Second, it will become very clear what you need to do. You will know which five or six marquee industry conferences your ideal customer attends every year. You will know who the influencers are in the industry. You will know the few places you need to be and the countless ones you shouldn't pay even a second's thought to.

Just as surfers have their favorite locations off their favorite beaches, the Separate group is where you will find the best waves.

You're in the ocean, my friend. You separated out your niche, and it looks to me like there is a wave moving toward you. Time to start paddling, while still looking over your shoulder. We'll paddle softly at first, because we will be measuring the wave as we Unify with it. Then, as the wave gets closer, we will paddle harder and harder.

WHAT IF YOU DON'T HAVE MANY (OR ANY) CUSTOMERS?

When I started my first business, I had zero customers and a business plan I scrawled on a cocktail napkin while drinking my problems away at Applebee's. My main goal was to show my boss I could do a better job than he could by opening my own business. I wasn't thinking about trends, or what qualities a top client would have. I just wanted clients!

If you're just starting out and have very few clients, or none at all, I suggest you begin by studying review sites like Yelp. Find your competition on the sites, but don't be so concerned about the ratings or what the reviews say. Instead, focus on the people making the comments. Try to learn about them, get a sense of their demographics. This is a sample of *your* future customers, and there is knowledge to be gained here.

As a quick example, I do this for myself with my books. First, I go on Amazon and look at competing books. I then go to the reviews, not so much to see what they are saying as much as who is saying it. Some of the folks post their contact information in their profiles. I reach out and ask if they are interested in reading one of my draft manuscripts and giving critical feedback. Talk about engaging the early adopters! The folks have already proven to be vocal about books, and since they help me define my book, they often become vocal supporters when the book is released.

Meet with noncompeting businesses that you believe are targeting the same market. For example, if you are setting up technology for your clients, try to find an app developer who makes products for the same clients that you are building the technology for and gain insight on the customer base from them.

And of course, you can always try to meet with a company that does exactly what you do, but is serving a different geographic market. If you're opening a small restaurant in New York City, interview a small restaurant owner in Chicago. You're not a threat to them and, as is human nature, they will likely share advice. Because we all like to talk about ourselves.

ACTION STEPS

1. When it comes to a niche focus you can almost never be too specific, but you can surely be too broad. Answer yes to these three questions about your niche, and you are likely focused enough:

   a. If you sell to other businesses, is there a dominant (as in *one*) type of association specifically for this group? Or, if you sell to consumers, is there a dominant (as in *one*) type of club or meetup specifically for this group?

   b. Would you or your industry message make you an obvious keynote speaker for this group?

   c. If you list the one hundred top influencers in the niche, would all of them know each other? And would they all want to know of you?

2. Join the association or group for your niche and, most importantly, participate. I mean schedule a year of *never* missing a gathering with that group. Then do it again next year.

3. Write a one-page bulleted list of topics, angles, and arguments that demonstrate how what you do is important to the transitioning needs of your niche community. Chances are you will be keynoting (or doing something similar) shortly.

4. Follow through on Step 1 and actually identify the one hundred top influencers in your niche. Track their names and their contact info, where they go and what they do. Go all FBI on them and network with them like mad. The social network this will reveal is your gateway to being an industry authority.

UNIFY

4

THE STORY OF JOHN CHAPMAN HAS CONTINUED IN FOLKLORE for centuries. The eccentric wanderer who was known for wearing a saucepan on his head planted apple trees throughout the American frontier. Of course you don't know him as John Chapman. You know him as Johnny Appleseed. Chances are that your perception of Johnny Appleseed is as a goofy do-gooder, enriching the American landscape with apple trees. But the real story of John "Johnny Appleseed" Chapman is in his masterful application of SURGE.

A native of Pittsburgh, which at the time was a launch point for American settlers to move west into the Ohio River Valley and beyond, Chapman spotted a consistent behavior in his niche—his marketplace wave. The growing stream of settlers moving into Pennsylvania and other neighboring states were thirsty for something. Literally. In his book *The Botany of Desire*, author Michael Pollan points out that the settlers needed relief from the stresses of frontier life: diseases, hard labor, brutal weather, constant threats. They also needed a bacteria-free drink, an alternative to the water that was often unsafe to drink.

Chapman found a way to unify with his marketplace wave (settlers seeking an alternative to water) by providing the perfect elixir: apple cider. It wasn't the kind of cider you get with a graham cracker at snack time. Johnny had gallons and gallons of the hard stuff (hic). And now you know why Johnny Appleseed wore that pot on his head. He was wasted.

Unifying his botanical skill with the needs of new settlers also allowed Chapman a side benefit. In the push to get settlers to move westward, frontier law allowed them to lay claim to land simply by establishing a permanent homestead, a claim that could be substantiated at the time by planting fifty apple trees to create a functioning orchard. Once his orchards were established and his land claims secure, he would sell or lease his orchards to new settlers and move on to establish more.

Chapman continued to make his signature cider as he led the push westward with his orchards, and he had a nice stiff drink waiting for new settlers as they followed in his wake. Where a separated group (in this case, the men and women settlers who were moving west) expresses a growing need or desire (in this case, a safe way to get fluids while gaining relief from the daily hardships of colonial life) that matches your unique skills, talents, and passion (planting thriving apple orchards), you Unify with the marketplace. This is where good things—and in Johnny Appleseed's case, good times—happen. By the time Chapman died at the age of seventy, he still owned more than twelve hundred acres in the Midwest. Chapman mastered being at the right place at the right time and repeated the formula over and over again. Perfectly.

You've identified your own "settlers" in the Separate stage. The next stage in the SURGE process is to do the U, Unify. By closely studying your settlers, you will determine *how* they are moving, in what direction they are heading, and where you can plant your "apple seeds" to stay immediately in front of their needs. Now is the time to hone your offerings to suit your niche and get in sync with that rising wave.

YOU CAN'T BE ALL THINGS

"But wait a minute, Mike," you say, "have *you* been sippin' bad cider? I've got *several* services that will help my key customers!

Plus, my competitors have way more products than I do, so I *have* to sell more products. More things for more clients—that's what will give me the edge."

Here's the deal, Bob. That "do more for more's sake" mentality got you reading this book in the first place. If it was working, you would have written the book, and I would be reading it. Perhaps your book could be titled *Entrepreneurial Prostitution: How to Do Anything for Any Customer at Practically Any Price*. I know, that was a low blow, but I've got to wake you up. You've got to triple your efforts to focus even more narrowly now as you enter the Unify stage. You've got limited resources—limited money, limited time, limited manpower, and limited energy—to make this all work. Those resources equate to your ability to paddle, to put yourself in position to catch your wave. And you can only surf one wave at a time, remember, Bobby?

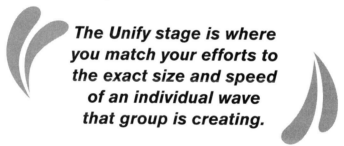

The Unify stage is where you match your efforts to the exact size and speed of an individual wave that group is creating.

Let's go back to your Separated group of clients. (Again, this is familiar territory for my *Pumpkin Plan* readers, but a necessary step in the SURGE process.) This niche you've separated will have a defined set of needs, desires, pressures, and requirements. And just as a wave has its own size and speed, so does your marketplace. If the Separate stage is the specific location in the ocean you are surfing, then the Unify stage is where you match your efforts to the exact size and speed of an individual wave that group is creating. Each need your niche has is a wave; every solution they seek, every requirement they have, is a wave. You now need to tune your unique solution to perfectly match one of these waves.

Think back to Brian Smith's story. In the Separate stage, he identified California surfers as the ideal customers for his UGG boots. Then, in the Unify stage, he identified their need to have warm feet while still looking "cool." That was his wave: California surfers who wanted to look cool while they warmed their feet. It doesn't seem like much, but you now know how Brian rode that one small wave to billions in revenue.

 *Each one of those needs, desires, pressures, and requirements is a wave, and each one is an opportunity to be surfed.*

As I build Profit First Professionals, my organization for progressive accounting professionals, I identify needs this group has, such as mastering the ever-changing technology and tools of their industry. I become an expert in their desires, such as connecting and sharing with peers, and their pressures, such as transitioning from transactional work (data entry) to advisory work (guiding clients). And I know their industry requirements, such as the use of accounting software. Each one of those needs, desires, pressures, and requirements is a wave, and each one is an opportunity to be surfed.

FurtherEd is unified and surfing hard on the wave of mastering the ever-changing technology and skill requirements needed by bookkeeping and accounting professionals. Woodard Consulting and The Sleeter Group are the two pro companies carving up the wave of peer-to-peer connection, sharing, and education for these accountants. Many more—Sage, Xero, Intuit, Wave, and Freshbooks— are riding different parts of the accounting software wave. And me? Profit First Professionals is focused on giving the step-by-step for bookkeepers and accountants to transition from data entry clerks to highly-regarded profitability advisors, practically overnight.

FIND YOUR WAVE IN FIVE

So, what about your Separate group? How do *you* find the waves that are forming in your marketplace? Easy: You ask.

The plan is simple. You want to identify five common elements of your niche marketplace:

1. Problems
2. Pressures
3. Needs
4. Requirements
5. Desires

Once you've identified these five commonalities, you then Unify them with your unique business solution.

Let's start by clearly identifying the wave you will Unify with. The process is as follows:

First, interview your best customers—those you identified in the last chapter. Meet with them face to face. Even if you are in a B2C company, you can still do this with a few dozen of your best customers. Once you're in front of these key customers, start asking questions. But not the "What do you want?" and "What can I do better?" questions that actually make things more confusing. Instead, ask very specific, Jedi mind-trick, truth-getting questions:

1. What specific elements of my company's services or products are best?
2. What about my industry is wrong or frustrating?
3. What are the biggest frustrations or challenges you are facing?

Here is the Jedi power in each of those questions (be ready, Bob, I mean, Luke):

WHAT SPECIFIC ELEMENTS OF MY COMPANY'S SERVICES OR PRODUCTS ARE BEST?

When your customers tell you what is best about your service or product, they in fact *won't* be telling you what is best. They will be telling you what they are paying the most attention to and what you must improve to really wow them. How do you like that move?

Just to make sure you get it, I will share an example. When I asked this question of my hedge fund client while I was building my first business, a tech support company, the managing partner said, "Your company responds quickly to computer problems and always has someone on-site within a few hours. That's impressive." Even if he didn't realize it, his answer was not telling me that quick response times were what was best about my business. Instead he was telling me that the *most critical* thing I can *improve* for him is my response time. And that's what I did. No surprise, once I figured out a way to have my technicians at his office in less than an hour after a reported problem—and later, as technology improved, *immediately* after the problem was reported, he noticed. Not only did he notice; he was thrilled. But I knew he would be, because he told me he would by sharing where he paid the most attention.

Ask your top customers what they like most about you, and they will in fact tell you what you need to improve.

WHAT ABOUT MY INDUSTRY IS WRONG OR FRUSTRATING?

If you and I were having lunch together, and a little bit of dry spit was piling up in the corner of my mouth, chances are you would rather avoid looking at me and choke down your food, than say, "Hey Mike, you have this disgusting white blob of crust on your face. Go wipe it off!" Why are you unlikely to say something? Because it's not socially appropriate. It's downright uncomfortable and awkward to say something. (As a side note, the next time you and I meet, make sure you ask me about the Copenhagen unibrow experience I had. It is the most fascinating, albeit embarrassing, experience I have had with "socially uncomfortable" behavior.)

That question, "What is wrong with my industry?" removes the uncomfortable feeling. Why? Because the conversation is about someone who is not in the room. Just as if crust-face weren't me, but the guy two tables over. You and I would be whispering back and forth about how embarrassing it is to be him. He couldn't hear us, so we'd disparage away. Same is true with business. If you ask your best customers what's wrong with your company, very few (read that as no one) will tell you the honest truth, because it's socially uncomfortable. But when you ask, "What's wrong with my industry?" you are now talking about old crust-face down the road. With that, the truth comes out. And what is frustrating and wrong with your industry is exactly what you need to address for your business. Powerful stuff, Luke. But this next one is going to blow your mind. Like, "I am your father" type blow your mind.

WHAT ARE THE BIGGEST CHALLENGES OR FRUSTRATIONS YOU ARE FACING?

This final question starts to "peel back the onion," so be prepared to ask a lot more "why" questions after you get your initial answer. For example, the coffee shop customer might say, "I get so frustrated by the seam on paper coffee cups." But what's wrong with having a seam? All paper cups have seams. Is this customer against paper cups in general? Is she seam-o-phobic? You don't know, so you need to dig deeper with a "why" question. When you ask, "Why are you frustrated by the seam?" you find out that the coffee drips down the seam and onto your customer's clothing when she's drinking it. The problem is dripping coffee cups, not seams, necessarily. You need to solve the drip, and the solution may be a better lid, or better cups, or trousers made out of sponge. You're not looking for the customer to solve the problem; you are looking for waves. The unique solution that you come up with is, in part, how you ride that wave. Use these three questions as your starting point. But dive as deep as you can with all the questions necessary to find the commonality of the problems, pressures, needs, requirements, and desires your best customers have.

KNOW YOUR WAVE

Since we're talking quite a bit about focusing your efforts on a highly specific niche, and giving one hundred percent to the effort, it's important to acknowledge that we're doing a bit of prediction here in the Unify stage. You've gathered a good deal of information during the Separate phase that should lead you to make a highly educated guess on where the industry is moving, but in the end it is just that: a guess.

When I met surfing pro Holly Beck, she told me that she isn't always right about every wave. "Even the best-looking wave in the world may be a dud. You never know the quality of a wave until you pop up on it." But there is a difference between ocean waves and marketplace waves that works to your advantage. In business, you can get feedback from others who have already seen a wave go past them.

Remember when we talked about history repeating? The niche you are trying to serve has been around a long time, probably a hell of a lot longer than you, and there is knowledge to be gleaned from that history. Now that you know more about what your customers want and need, look to the history of *their* industry for clues about trends that could repeat and determine if these trends, modified for modern times, would be useful to your target customer.

Everything moves in cycles, just like tides. The specifics may change, but if you really study the market (and you must), you'll start to see the same stories coming around time after time. The old

Ford Mustang from the 1960s is back in modernized form today. The once-popular six hundred-pound bearded lady sideshow at the amusement park is now *My 600-lb. Life*, a hit reality TV show on TLC. The snake oil salesman peddling the elixir that solves everything, fast, is now an internet marketer (ouch!). What was once, will be again.

As you attempt to time the marketplace wave based on history, you want to seek out actual instances of history repeating. Just because panniers—hoop petticoats women used to wear to make their dresses wide as doorways, or, if they were really wealthy, wider—were big when our boy Johnny Appleseed was born doesn't mean petticoats are coming back big *this* fashion season and you should go all in. Not at all; but you should be on the watch for it.

As you attempt to time the marketplace wave based on history, you want to seek out actual instances of history repeating.

Corsets, on the other hand, were hot a few decades after panniers, and they're back again with a modern spin. The 18th-century corset was a conical fabric undergarment that women wore to give themselves V-shaped torsos. Simply pull tightly on the lacing (and, often, break a few ribs) and these women looked great (even if they didn't *feel* great). Enter Spanx. Soon after Spanx launched in 2000, Neiman Marcus picked up the product line in seven stores. Consumers quickly started buying this modern twist on the old corset, and Spanx was surfing the massive wave of women—and some men—who wanted to change the way their body looked. The energy source of wanting to look good has always been around; this was just a new single wave of a specific way women wanted to do it—via a body shape-changing garment.

The next wave in looking-good fashion? Could it be the return of the dickey? Not.

ALIGN VS. PIVOT

There are some basic rules to surfing. Purely for your own health, you try to ride waves that your talents, experience, and skill level match. As Owen Mulford, the cofounder of Billabong's OC Groms Surf School (say that ten times fast) in Ocean City, Maryland, explained, on your first few times out trying to catch waves, you'll learn the most and be safest if you surf the small, close waves that have already broken. You're not going to insanely carve it up with that type of wave, but you probably won't have your board kick back and smack you in the face, either. And no matter what, as Owen always says, "Stay stoked."

Here the analogy between ocean surfing and marketplace surfing only goes so far, because in marketplace surfing, you can quickly jump from riding one wave to another, and if you do it right, you can carve right off a starter wave and grab a monster wave with a simple twist, turn, and alignment.

One of my closest friends is Jabe (pronounced "jay-bee") Blanchard, founder of RoofDeck Solutions. If you know him, he is one of your best friends, too. Jabe is just that type of warm soul. But even if you don't know him, you need to know how he unified with his marketplace wave.

RoofDeck Solutions started (with a different corporate name) by selling materials to outdoor contractors who were building everything from patios to pools and, as his business grew, it also splintered. The materials and knowledge needed for building ground-level patios are vastly different than those needed for residential decks, and both of those niches are entirely different than that of building urban decks, which are often located on the roofs of buildings. Too many waves, and only so many resources, remember? So Jabe aligned his company to ride one wave. He picked his favorite customer niche, urban decks, and matched it to his passion for construction and environmental responsibility.

Aligning is different than pivoting. When you pivot your business based on what your customer wants you to do, you cater to their needs (that's good), but not necessarily yours (that's bad). If you simply pivot based on what your customer wants, it makes it nearly impossible to unify your people behind the effort, because you and your team didn't sign up to surf *that* wave. Growing a business is hard enough. Who wants to work to grow something they don't really have their heart in?

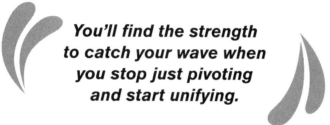

You'll find the strength to catch your wave when you stop just pivoting and start unifying.

But when you cater to your customer's needs (that's still good) *and* your needs, desires, and dreams (now you're talking), you're riding the perfect board for the perfect wave. RoofDeck did it, and they became the Big Kahuna in a small niche practically overnight. Jabe is known as an industry innovator, bringing new technology to the roofing industry. He is so unified with his desire, and his customers' desires, that he rapidly achieved global recognition. Most recently, his firm was awarded the largest roof deck project ever to occur in the Bahamas, even though thousands of local contractors could do an adequate job. See? He's still surfing those waves—and loving every second of it. Don't just pivot. Align.

You'll find the strength to catch your wave when you stop just pivoting and start unifying. First, have a clear definition of what *you* want. Instead of the ineffective, it's-worked-for-nobody strategy of "I want to get rich doing what I hate, so I can then go do what I love," start with passion and purpose and stick with it. Define a business purpose that *feeds your soul*. Then adjust to customer demand and marketplace shifts. Adapt to what your best customers want, but *always* ensure that you are unified with your purpose. You can pivot your way into a business that makes money, but makes you sick; or you can unify your business into something that makes money *and* makes you happy. That's when you have your version of RoofDeck Solutions. And I understand what Jabe loves about his business, because the view from one of those gorgeous decks high up in a New York City building (or a premier resort in the Bahamas) will bring tears to your eyes.

Listen to the wants of your best customers and adjust to serve them, while simultaneously listening to the needs of your heart and staying true to it. That's unification. That's profit first and a wealthy soul.

AND SOMETIMES YOU PIVOT

Donna Leyens discovered her niche in a way that a lot of business owners do—by recognizing a need that she herself had, and then developing a solution. Donna became a business coach in 2009, marrying her skills as a certified coach with her passion for supporting entrepreneurs and small innovative businesses. Over the years, she noticed a few things about her chosen industry: number one, business coaching was an undefined term that could have many meanings (and not always flattering); two, not all business coaches had training or certification in coaching (hence the not-so-flattering reputation those coaches earned); three, most coaching organizations lumped a wide variety of modalities under the term "business coaching," and four, most training was not relevant to small business coaching in the first place. As a result, most business coaches who focused on working with entrepreneurs and small business owners were independent professionals struggling to make a living.

In 2012, Donna and I partnered to found Provendus Group to turn my book *The Pumpkin Plan* into a licensed business coaching system, with the aim of producing amazing growth results for clients and helping small business coaches build their own profitable coaching businesses. But as she started to implement the Pumpkin Plan in Provendus, Donna ran into an obstacle. One of the key strategies in the Pumpkin Plan is Concentric Circle Marketing. Basically, you figure out where your niche market "hangs out" and then you show up there. Donna said, "When I started looking for organizations and conferences that catered specifically to small business coaches, I came up empty."

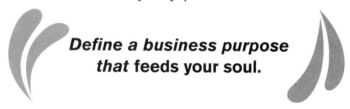

Define a business purpose that feeds your soul.

While she searched for concentric circles, Donna worked with small business coaches day to day. She soon realized that there were many more ways she could support them in their business growth than just providing them with a licensed product. Then, the light bulb went on. Don't you just love it when that happens? I do. Donna sure does! She told me, "I realized that if I couldn't find the business or organization I was looking for, I could start it myself!"

Donna decided to pivot. Today, she is launching and growing The Entrepreneur's Coach Alliance. Her goal is to unite the small business coaching industry, and her Rally Cry (which we will discuss in the next chapter) is to save small businesses from extinction. Now, she has created the organization she was hoping to join, with full support of the very people she wants to serve. You see, they were looking for the same organization. There was a need. A void. And Donna plans to fill it. Stage One (S): complete. Stage Two (U): underway. Stage Three (R): is, as you can see, being formulated.

WHAT IF YOU DON'T HAVE MANY (OR ANY) CUSTOMERS?

When my friend David Schnurman took over Lawline in 2007, the company brought in around ten thousand bucks in annual revenue. By the end of 2015, Lawline broke five million, and it is poised to blaze right past six million in 2016.

Founded by David's father, Alan Schnurman, Lawline provided continuing education for attorneys, who are required to take a certain number of ongoing classes in order to maintain their licenses. David was in law school when he took over the company.

"What I really wanted to do was start my own law firm," David told me over the phone the other day. "But when I looked out in the marketplace and saw all of these TED talks and other information out there for entrepreneurs starting businesses, I couldn't find one in a simplified format for the law."

David decided to create the content he was looking for and up-level the quality. "In the past, courses for attorneys were in CD format, or a live space with four older men sitting on a dais with bad lighting and even worse sound. We created high production-quality videos that were more personal and more interesting. Right away, that resonated with our customers and our faculty."

Even though Lawline had very few customers in 2007, David had other people he could interview to discover the five common elements of his niche marketplace: its problems, pressures, needs, requirements, and desires. He had his dad, and his law school buddies, and he had *himself.* David could use himself as a source for the information he needed to figure out how to unify his product with current and prospective clients.

"Attorneys are so pressed for time," David said. "When we built Lawline, our whole focus was on freedom. Freedom to get credits done as fast as possible, for the best value. Freedom to grow your practice. And for our faculty, freedom to get exposure."

If you don't have top clients yet, or any clients, find friends or family members who may be part of your demographic and ask them. If you come up empty, try interviewing clients you would like to have. Reach out by phone or email. At the very least, ask *yourself.*

Once Lawline started to attract attention for its improved quality, it started attracting more and better faculty who wanted more exposure. Exposure meant attorneys could get in front of more prospective clients—corporate attorneys who often outsource some services, and attorneys who refer their clients to other attorneys who specialize in different areas of law. He realized that there were two benefactors for his offering: the consumer, who is required by law to continue training, and the teacher, who wants more exposure. Then, he adjusted his offering to not only serve the consumer, but also the teacher. Lawline's base offer is consumer-focused, providing a variety of high-quality content at a low price. For the teachers, David built a platform so they could get massive exposure. "It used to be that you had fifty people in a room. We improved distribution and made it possible for attorneys to get exposure to thousands for one class."

David helped attorneys become rock stars. One of his faculty members would be in China walking to a courthouse, for example, and run into a Lawline student. People would stop these attorneys and say, "Oh my God, you're (so and so). I saw you on Lawline." David's faculty lawyers began to be seen as the elite. If you wanted to get in front of the general counsel at a big firm, Lawline was now the perfect pulpit.

Today, Lawline is the largest provider of continuing education for attorneys. They have thousands of teachers working with them, and more than 130,000 attorneys have taken their courses. Out of the Fortune 500 companies, more than 400 use Lawline for continuing education. All of the top financial firms use Lawline, and almost all of the Fortune 100 companies.

"Every attorney is an expert in something," David added. "The more we can facilitate knowledge sharing between attorneys, customers and faculty, the more it builds on itself. That has made us successful over the years—creating such great content and having so many attorneys creates momentum."

David spotted the wave by asking himself—and the attorneys he knew—what they wanted. That initial spark of an idea, to provide a simplified format for attorneys to build their firms, was born of his own need to find that information. Building Lawline, David took the idea further and provided attorneys with a platform from which they could build their firms. He spotted the wave, and Lawline is riding it all the way to the bank.

ACTION STEPS

1. Set up interviews with at least three of your top clients. Prepare your questions in advance. Don't skip this step! Schedule it now. They can point you directly to the wave you want to ride.

2. Take note of commonalities in your clients' answers. Which of their problems or desires is your company uniquely suited to solve?

3. Of the solutions you could provide to your clients, which of these are they most interested in? Don't guess. Ask them. Now, which do you enjoy most? Don't gloss over this. Dive deep until you find a soulful answer.

RALLY

5

DO YOU FEEL IT LIFTING YOU UP? THE WAVE IS UPON YOU.

You chose your surfing spot during the Separate stage. You spotted the wave you want to ride and you have been paddling hard to get aligned in front of it during the Unify stage. Now, in the Rally stage, you are going to pop up on it. The energy is about to shift from you doing all the work to the wave carrying you.

This is a tough transition, since what got you here was hard paddling and what will get you the rest of the way is hard carving. Those are distinctly different skills. Paddling is raw energy and muscle. Carving is turning and twisting, coupled with maintaining balance and, of course, a little bit (or a lotta bit) of showmanship. Paddling is exerting energy. Carving is capturing it.

The Rally stage is all about how you get up and ride the wave. You're not going anywhere by just floating around in circles, flapping your arms, and claiming to be "unique." You gain momentum from the incoming wave by tailoring what you do best to what your customers need most, then combining those two into a focused, unique solution.

Why is this difference so important? Because, in the eyes of your customers and clients, better is *not* better, *different* is better. Highlight and tattoo that one too, would ya? Prospects are blind to better. They won't value that you answer the phone faster, that your website is easier to navigate, or that your people are friendlier. Those are all good things, but with the three seconds of attention your prospect will give you, just being better won't do it. Being *different* will.

The Cronut® wasn't an attempt to make a better donut, or even a better croissant, for that matter. It was an attempt to create something *different*. Uber wasn't a better taxi service; it was a different

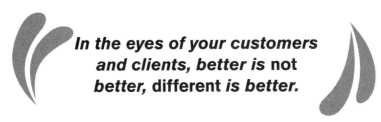

In the eyes of your customers and clients, better is **not** *better,* **different** *is better.*

one. The Vibram FiveFingers shoe wasn't an attempt to make a better Nike. It was a different spin on a running shoe. And the HOKA ONE ONE shoe is the newest and most different alternative to the Vibram. *Get it?*

The method to Rally is simple: Be the only one of your type riding the wave, make your differences supremely clear, and the wave will take notice and carry you.

When I started looking for the surge in my own businesses, I needed some help. I'd been practicing the Separate and Unify stages for years, but now I was about to enter new territory. It wasn't that I didn't know that different is better. I had been practicing differentiation for a while. But my attempts at clearly conveying to my customer base how my company was different were a bit like throwing spaghetti at a wall. Sometimes the approach stuck; sometimes it was a soggy noodle that dropped to the floor.

Rallying your peeps is not always easy. I feel your pain. I did nail it eventually, and then everything clicked. And I don't just mean with my customers—I mean everything clicked with *me*.

THE RALLY CRY

Defining your uniqueness is what the Rally stage of SURGE is all about. You need to simply and easily define what unique solution you offer, in your unique way, to your unique set of customers. Your unique offer matched to your unique voice for a very specific target customer wave is more than an elevator pitch; it's your *Rally Cry.* (My editors informed me that the correct grammar is actually "Rallying Cry," but it doesn't exactly roll off the tongue, does it? So, I'm going with "Rally Cry," and I'll willingly take my punishment from the grammar police.)

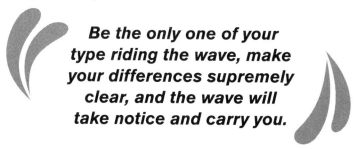

Be the only one of your type riding the wave, make your differences supremely clear, and the wave will take notice and carry you.

Your Rally Cry starts with a term or phrase that uniquely speaks to your community. As Simon Sinek explains in his book *Start with Why,* this is the greater purpose for your business's existence beyond just making money. It is your own unique way of expressing your why. Done right, it will fuel your customers to flock to your side and support your rapid growth in the market.

As I shared with you before, my company, Profit First Professionals, is an international organization of accountants, bookkeepers, and business experts who have the unique training and skills to maximize your company's profits. Maybe that statement explaining who we are and what we do has you intrigued, but I suspect that it didn't strike the "Aha! This organization is for me" chord. But our Rally Cry might just invoke that feeling with you. Let's try it on for size… *Eradicate entrepreneurial poverty.* Did that connect? Did you just "get it" without further explanation? If so, you are likely part of our Separated community. If the statement didn't land, you're not.

That is the purpose of the Rally Cry. It concisely states your company's greater purpose while simultaneously speaking the unique language of your Separated community and filtering out everyone else. Simply communicating your Rally Cry constantly and consistently becomes your greatest sales tool.

The Rally Cry for Life is Good® is built right into the company name. Either you get it and belong, or you don't and you don't. Jet Blue's Rally Cry is "Up for good." Dr. Martin Luther King, Jr.'s was "All men are created equal." Your Rally Cry is the impact you intend to have on others. Say it simply, say it boldly, say it often, and your community—the Separated group—will rally around you. A Rally Cry is more than the purpose you serve; it is the unifying motivator. When your community hears it, they are reminded of their commitment and are ready to roll. Just watch the Marines shout their famous Rally Cry "Ooh-rah!" and you will know what I mean. "Ooh-rah" is steeped with meaning, reminds Marines of their loyalty to each other, and invokes a call to action. If you are a Marine, you get it; if you're not, you don't.

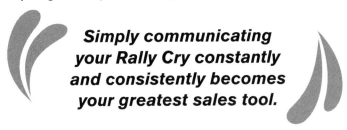

> **Simply communicating your Rally Cry constantly and consistently becomes your greatest sales tool.**

The first Californian surfer who walked down the beach in the 1980s in a pair of sheepskin UGGs must have looked like a weirdo. Other surfers must have thought, "That guy took one too many hits from the ganja pipe this morning and decided to dress in a pair of Dan Aykroyd's *Spies Like Us* boots." The transition point from paddling to the wave pushing you is when the early adopters take the "risk" of committing to you. In order for those brave souls to rally around you, you need to prepare them accordingly with a purpose. UGG's Rally Cry was not "warm feet;" that is the benefit of wearing the boots. UGG's Rally Cry for surfers was that surfers should be able to "Catch a wave any day," no matter how cold it was.

YOUR RALLY CRY

Ever watch your favorite team play a major game? Your team stands for something. Honor or revenge. Perfection or respect. Beating Goliath. Going undefeated. Representing your town, city, or country. The list of possible Rally Cries goes on and on. Your team inevitably has a chant, saying, or cheer—self-assigned or crowd-created—that speaks to the team's stance. So what is the phrase or sound that your fans (customers) use to bond around your company's purpose?

You don't start with the words; you start with your purpose and the Rally Cry becomes obvious. Your company's purpose is defined via a succinct phrase that you, your company, and your community revolve around. For my business, Profit First Professionals, the purpose is to "guide entrepreneurs to once and for all keep some of the money their company makes, and as a result bring stability and confidence to them." Super clunky, right? It doesn't roll off the tongue. Try saying it in a loud voice with enthusiasm. Not effective. It's our purpose, but it isn't a Rally Cry yet.

For me, coming up with a Rally Cry was a bit similar to coming up with a subtitle for one of my books. I always start out with this long sentence that sounds a lot like "and, and, and." My writing partner, Anjanette Harper, does her best to rein me in, and then I come back with an even longer sentence. She reminds me that the subtitle had to succinctly convey the promise of the book—not the kitchen sink.

As we worked on drilling down to our Rally Cry for Profit First Professionals, over time, it slowly and naturally turned into

"Eradicate entrepreneurial poverty." That is a statement that encapsulates everything we were trying to say in our longer, clunky statement, but it's much more powerful. And it is a Rally Cry that fits with my entire work/life mission. It's not just the Rally Cry for PFP; it's the Rally Cry for Mike Michalowicz. This is the message that I shout from the rooftops. This is the message that beats with the drum of my heart. This is the message that got me out of bed at the ass-crack of dawn to write this book.

But enough about me. What do you stand for? And why?

1. **A better way.** Your customers, community and/or colleagues deserve something that makes their lives better or easier.
2. **A common enemy ideology.** A stand for a new belief, while defeating or overcoming an established belief.
3. **A common enemy competitor.** Generally, people like the underdogs and dislike the big player by default. Who is the established big player *you* are taking on and trying to take down?
4. **The great equalizer.** Only rich or connected people could have this thing in the past, but now you make it available to the common man.
5. **Only for the elite.** The rich and connected people have earned what you're offering. What you are doing for them is their reward for their hard work or good fortune.

In 1997, Apple solidified their position among creatives with their ad campaign centered around the slogan "Think Different." Talk about a Rally Cry. If you felt like an oddball who thought differently from most people, Apple established a community designed just for you. Finally, you were accepted. If you were a "Crazy One" as Apple defined you in their iconic television spot, you now had a place to go. The Rally Cry bonds a community around an ideology, which in turn strengthens the community. You notice that the Rally Cry isn't a definition of the product or service; it speaks to emotion. It filters out those who don't fit, and attracts those who do. It channels the focus on which customers you will serve. It captures the energy of the wave.

Your Rally Cry, complemented with a shot of inoculation, will impel your customers to carry your message and lend you the benefit of the doubt when you make mistakes. In the world of marketing, the Holy Grail is compelling your customers to do the marketing for you. When the person paying you is also your biggest promoter, you know you've nailed your Rally Cry.

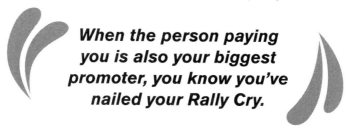

When the person paying you is also your biggest promoter, you know you've nailed your Rally Cry.

A Rally Cry is a repeatable, viral message that speaks to your mission and inspires the next prospect to become your customer. "Eradicate entrepreneurial poverty" is a Rally Cry that explains the reason for my company's existence, but also inspires customers to join us. Effectively, the Rally Cry is also a qualifier or filter. If you "get it," you have a reason to join us. If you don't get it, you move on.

So how do you create your Rally Cry? Here are a few powerful but simple steps:

1. First, get clarity on the purpose of your company. This purpose is far beyond money and status; it is the impact of what you are doing. It is how you serve customers and how you serve the world. If you don't have a mission for your business yet, start with yourself. What is *your* life purpose? How do you want to make an impact on the

world? Start with yourself, because when your life purpose is in alignment with your company's mission, then you can stand behind your Rally Cry—and your customers will hear it and stand by your company. When your personal and business missions are in sync, it is a beautiful thing. That's when your business becomes your soul mate, the ultimate platform and amplifier for you. I teach this in *The Toilet Paper Entrepreneur*. If you really want to dive deep into your mission, read *Start With Why* by Simon Sinek.

2. Next, cut that Rally Cry down to size. Inevitably, when people start brainstorming about their missions, they end up with full-fledged mission statements. What you want is one sentence; five words or less is ideal. You will start with one paragraph, or more. That's okay and expected. This means you have more than one Rally Cry hidden in that statement. You may think you don't, but if you have more than one paragraph, I guarantee there is more than one idea there. Spend time refining that statement until you have just one succinct message. You need to be able to say it quickly and be understood, no explanation required. This is one step for which you would benefit from working with a colleague or a friend. But know this: Your Rally Cry isn't right until it gives you goose bumps every time you hear it.

3. Once you've zeroed in on your Rally Cry, you must become the drum. Keep beating the rhythm; keep sounding the cry. Drop it in conversation. Write a manifesto about it and post it on your company's website. Print it out and post it on the wall in your office. Print it on the back of your business cards. Add it to your email signature. Remind people every chance you get that this is what you stand for. It takes some effort to spark interest in prospects, but

once you do, the Rally Cry will catch fire and do the work for you. Keep beating that drum. Do it in interviews, on video, in speeches, on your blog, on podcasts, in emails to prospects, in your Twitter bio—everywhere you can.

4. Your next step is to find your fanatics. Every business has a list of their most loyal customers, the fantastic fanatics who will do anything for the company. They are easy to find, because they are the people who raise their hands every time—and I do mean *every time*—you need help or have a question. Empower your fanatics to start beating the drum. Encourage them to follow your lead and engage in their own version of shouting the Rally Cry.

5. Once you've empowered your fans, make it easy for them to keep banging the drum. I never rely much on big names to promote me during my book launches. Instead, I engage the support of my biggest fans. I called them Buzz Warriors. Other people call their groups of diehard fans "street teams." I gave my Buzz Warriors the tools to help promote my book. Well in advance, I give them written content they can modify, contests they can promote, promo language to use, and other instructions. I make my goals clear, and I give them a way to talk to each other. The Buzz Warriors don't have to invent the rules or processes; their only job is to execute and spread the word. Which they do.

6. Once you've established your Rally Cry and have a team of people to help you spread it, start thinking about other methods for getting the word out. Stay on message, but come up with new themes, contests, events, and ways of presenting it. Life is Good is a perfect example. They have the same message, but they incorporate it into a constantly changing variety of clothing and products. If they had only had one T-shirt that said "Life is Good" and never

offered any variations, their company would never have made it. They don't stop there, of course; they have a massive annual Life is Good Festival, the Life is Good Kids Foundation, books, home products, pet products, and so much more. Do the same, over time, slowly. Find new ways to spread your Rally Cry.

7. Your Rally Cry doesn't have to be set in stone. While I don't recommend changing it until you've achieved your goals, you can create a new Rally Cry when it's time. You may find you need a new one in order to ride the next wave. You may also consider putting a deadline in your Rally Cry, which becomes a great motivator. For example, John F. Kennedy had several messages. One of his most memorable was "We will put a man on the moon by the end of the decade." Mission accomplished.

YOU DON'T WANT A MEGAPHONE, YOU WANT A DOG WHISTLE

Earlier in the chapter I mentioned Anjanette, my writing partner. For years, she told me she wanted to introduce me to her friend Dr. Venus Opal Reese, who, like me, speaks and writes about business. Anjanette insisted she was making a love connection. Turns out, she was right.

When we finally met and I asked Dr. Venus to tell me her backstory, she said simply, "I used to live on the streets; I graduated from Stanford with a second master's and a PhD; and I'm a Black woman millionaire."

We've all heard come-from-behind stories, but what I found fascinating about Dr. Venus's story was how she transformed her coaching and mentoring business by developing an authentic, impassioned Rally Cry that spoke to her target demographic. She also schooled me on appealing to everyone when I thought I had that down. Of course, that's when I fell in love with her. We'll get to that in a moment.

A former tenured professor at the University of Texas in Dallas, Dr. Venus started her coaching and mentoring business to supplement her income in the summer months. In the early days, she struggled to find clients who would pay her the big bucks. "My messaging sounded 'Black woman,' but I was marketing to white women because I was told that's where the money was," Dr. Venus told me. "Yet, when I looked at my high-ticket clients, people who were paying at least eighteen thousand a year to work with me, I noticed that eight out of ten of them were Black women who had a good education, a good job, and a side hustle. When I realized that, I changed everything. I started focusing solely on Black women. I Pumpkin-Planned it, Mike!"

(You may think this is when I fell in love with Dr. Venus—hearing people talk about zeroing in on top clients always makes my heart go all aflutter—but you'd be wrong. It's coming.)

"I turned all the survival methods I used on the streets—literally eating out of trash cans, sleeping in piss and beer in alleyways, that whole scene—I turned that pain into profit, and I began to teach Black women to do the same. Your million-dollar money-maker isn't located in your brain; it's located in your *pain*."

Dr. Venus explained that she organized her business model around three simple ideas: mess, million-dollar message, and movement. "My mess was, I transformed 'I'm a piece of shit' into 'I matter.' My message I transformed into 'We matter.' And my movement I transformed into 'Black women matter.' Then I created ten videos based on this movement for Black women business owners. The truth was so real, the women passed it around."

As soon as Dr. Venus zeroed in on her Rally Cry—Black women matter—clients flocked to her. "People don't buy from their heads, they buy from their hearts—their broken hearts," Dr. Venus said.

"If you make a heart connection to what they already believe, they will buy from you. I believe Black women matter, but no one is saying that. When I put that message on loudspeaker, what Black women already know to be true, I can rally my ladies around the truth."

Here's where I fell in love.

"I hear 'Black women matter' and I think, that makes sense, but it doesn't affect me," I said.

Dr. Venus started laughing. "It's not *supposed* to, Mike. Think about it."

Oh. *I'm* not her target demographic. I'm not top client material. Duh.

"I teach my clients about dog-whistle positioning," Dr. Venus said. "A dog whistle can only be heard by certain dogs. It's not supposed to be heard by people.

"I don't have a lot of clients. I have one hundred percent the right ones," she continued. "My people will fight for me. I have a tribe. If my systems break down, they will wait for me. If my technology fails, they will move with me to another platform. If I say I'm going to be on reality television, they will push it out. I was featured in *Forbes* and I sent out one email, one tweet and posted one update on Facebook. That article had twenty-eight thousand views. *That's* a tribe."

It's not that Dr. Venus excludes clients who are not Black women. In fact, she has Latina clients, white clients, even men. It's just that her Rally Cry is specific to Black women, and it resonates with those clients whose skin might not match, but hearts do. Still, I had to ask, "Are you worried about alienating people with your Rally Cry?"

"No, because I'm not interested in them. People who try to serve everyone don't know who they are. They twist themselves into pretzels trying to follow trends and appeal to everyone. I'm not trying to be Oprah. I have too much street in me. I'm only interested in the sisters who are willing to do the real work to be free. I feel like I'm fulfilling my destiny. For me to go from the street to Stanford to seven figures is a miracle. I live my work."

Her message resonated so strongly with me that I quipped, "I think we need to get married, Dr. Venus."

"No can do, Mike. I am not just a Black woman. I am a married Black woman who loves her wife."

"Now we absolutely have to. That is a headline that will surely get both our Rally Cries out!"

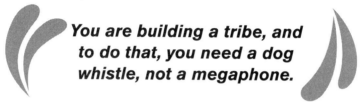

You are building a tribe, and to do that, you need a dog whistle, not a megaphone.

When creating your Rally Cry, you may be tempted to try to appeal to more than one demographic. At the very least, you will probably worry that your Rally Cry might offend or alienate someone. Don't worry about it. You are building a tribe, and to do that, you need a dog whistle, not a megaphone.

SHOUT FROM THE ROOFTOPS

Let's dig a little deeper into getting the message out. How do you get people to hear your Rally Cry? There are a number of ways. One way is to become a spokesperson for your new community and its beliefs. Tony Hsieh built Zappos to rally around excellent customer service, making himself the leader of a near cult-like customer following. He did speaking engagements about going to extremes to care for customers. He wrote a wildly popular book, *Delivering Happiness*, to show how Zappos was built around a corporate culture of happiness for employees and customers alike. And look at the book title... *Delivering Happiness*... it's a Rally Cry. Nicely done, Tony. Nicely done.

Elon Musk's most recent Rally Cry is to privatize space exploration. Kate Cole made her Rally Cry by combining Cinnabon treats and moderation—she has a community eating those sugar and carb concoctions like never before, yet readily suggests that you need to keep your Hooters physique through moderation. Yes, the CEO of Cinnabon had a lengthy career as a Hooters girl, moving on to management at the eatery chain and ultimately taking on her current position of CEO at Cinnabon.

I've done the same—the Rally Cry part, I mean. (I tanked my Hooters interview.) For my company, Profit First Professionals, I regularly share on radio, TV, and stage why the ideology of Sales - Expenses = Profit actually prevents most businesses from ever becoming profitable, and what to do about it. My Rally Cry is to eradicate entrepreneurial poverty by helping entrepreneurs take their profit first. And like Tony, my Rally Cry is built into my book's title: *Profit First*. You can do the same. How, and from where, will you shout your Rally Cry?

If you're not comfortable being the spokesperson yourself, you can build the support structure for other members of your company or leaders in your clients' community to carry the torch. eBay has masterfully empowered everyone to be an entrepreneur. If you have junk in your attic, you can rake in the cash within the next few hours selling it on the eBay platform. And who's the man yelling the Rally Cry from the rooftops? It's not so much John Donahoe, CEO of eBay, as it is Uncle Griff. Jim "Uncle Griff" Griffith is called the "Dean of eBay Education." More than knowing the eBay platform inside and out, more than knowing the purpose of eBay inside and out, Uncle Griff knows the eBay community inside and out because he *is* the community. Jim is one of them, and the rest of the community identifies with him. Find your Uncle Griff, your ultimate spokesperson, when you aren't it.

STRENGTH IN NUMBERS

The Rally phase also takes advantage of the strength in numbers that you foster when you bring people together. Most business owners I talk to are reluctant to connect their customers with each other out of fear that they will start comparing bad stories about the company. What really happens, actually, is the reverse. Once you connect your customers so that they can share stories, help each other through difficulties, and see that they are not the only customer you have, your customer community will actually work to reinforce the decisions each has made to do business with you. It's the psychology of people... we like to support each other.

Your clients will encourage each other (and you) in the early stages as you try to get up on the wave and ultimately build a stronger brand loyalty than they had before. Being part of a group helps people to reinforce their decision to work with you, and also empowers them to be ambassadors for your company, defending each other from naysayers.

Now that you have rallied your early-adopter customers together, it's time to gather everything you've learned from this first group of supporters and grab the full force of that wave. Your Rally customers will be with you, pushing you along and supporting you on the rough early stages of the ride.

WHAT IF YOU DON'T HAVE MANY (OR ANY) CUSTOMERS?

You don't have an excuse. Even if you don't have a single active customer, you have you. For your business to be wildly successful—both monetarily and in terms of purpose—it must feed your soul. (Yes, I am working on a book about this. It's one of the books in my "Sweet Spot" series.) Even sans a single customer, you can still have a Rally Cry. You still need to take that stance, even when you stand alone.

Ask yourself. Study yourself. Keep asking why your business exists, beyond just making money. Do you thirst for self-expression? Are you hoping to right a wrong? How are you going to stand up for yourself?

In the interesting, intertwined lives we lead, I have found that we need to give to others what we in fact need for ourselves. So my question is, what feeds your soul? Because there are countless souls out there hoping to be fed the same thing.

You may stand alone for a while, but they will join you. The Rally Cry will start to echo on its own. Want proof? Google "First Follower: Leadership Lessons from Dancing Guy" and you will see how a powerful community forms, even when—scratch that—*especially* when you start out by yourself.

ACTION STEPS

1. Brainstorm a Rally Cry. Working through the list of steps shared earlier in the chapter, come up with something your company stands for or against. Does it speak to your soul? No? Keep trying. Once you determine your company's Rally Cry, figure out how to convey it in five words or less.

2. Now think about how you would communicate that Rally Cry. Are you the most effective person to shout it? How can you make sure your best customers—and their clones—hear it?

3. Consider how you could bring your customers together. Could you create an online space for them to congregate? Or perhaps an in-person meetup, retreat, or conference?

4. You watched the Dancing Guy video, right? What?!?! You haven't?!?! Do it now. Do a web search for and watch "First Follower: Leadership Lessons from Dancing Guy." It is the ultimate Rally Cry and uses not a single word.

GATHER

"I JUST HEARD THAT TOUCAN!" I SAID. "THOSE BEASTS SQUAWK like a siren."

I mentioned surfing pro and model Holly Beck earlier in the book. I was on a Skype call with Holly, and she was connecting from her home in northern Nicaragua, so I thought it was entirely possible that a loud bird had chimed in from outside her window.

"Um, that was my daughter, Mike," Holly answered, as she picked up her baby girl and put her on her lap. Dang! I had just made the classic Skype faux pas: commenting on a sound when I couldn't see the culprit.

Holly knows more than most about the sport of surfing, having competed all over the world during her seven years on the pro circuit. Even now that she's given up competition and had a baby, Holly still continues to build her surf-based business, serving as a surfing ambassador for sponsors while leading surfing and yoga retreats. Even at an age when many of her peers have had to move on to other careers, Holly is still riding her SURGE.

"Once a surfer is up on a wave," I asked Holly, "how do they get the gnarliest ride?"

Holly then explained the surfer's version of what I call the Gather stage of SURGE. "Once you are up on the wave, you look for the pocket. You need to always know where it is, because that core of the wave has the most strength, height, and power. You can ride your board up and down the pocket for the entirety of the wave."

The pocket. The core of the wave. That is exactly it. The best, strongest, and longest ride comes from a *specific spot* on the wave. Now that you are up on the wave, you need to find the pocket and stay in it. For our purposes, the pocket of the SURGE is that spot where surging demand from a specific customer (your niche) meets your specialized skill (your niche offering) and where you continue to perfect that offering to *über-cater* to your niche. You do this by asking better questions of your customers and of your company. And by making adjustments to your offering whenever it is out of alignment with your core.

Riding in the pocket is the timing strategy on hyperspeed. You regularly seek out what your best customers need from you; improve, tweak, or overhaul your offering to meet that need; and then perfect it. Immediately following—or even during—the process, look for what your core needs most from you now. This constant and continuous improvement around what your best clients need is how you stay in the pocket of the marketplace wave.

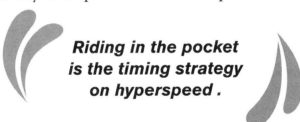

Riding in the pocket is the timing strategy on hyperspeed .

Unfortunately for many businesses, the Gather phase is often overlooked. You are up on the wave, after all, at least for a moment. Why not start showing off your moves? Because even though a wave can be massive, you are only riding a very small section of it, and that small section is always shifting.

"If you are going to get a good ride, you must *always* look for the pocket," Holly repeated.

A loud squawk sounded again. I said, "Your daughter is lively this morning, Holly."

"*That* was a toucan."

The wave is pushing you now. You should feel it. How do you know? When well-suited opportunities constantly come your way without any marketing effort. In other words, your current clients are singing your praises to other ideal prospects, just like them, and those prospects are so convinced that you are the one for them that they come right to you—automatically. As Ken Blanchard shares in *Raving Fans*, this only happens when existing customers have such an extraordinary experience with you that they feel compelled to tell everyone and their mothers about you.

The greatest way to give customers an extraordinary experience is to *anticipate* their needs. Highlight that one, too. When someone else anticipates our need and addresses it even before we are fully aware of it, it is damn impressive. It's legendary hockey player Wayne Gretzky's "move to where the puck is going" strategy, and it is the essence of SURGE.

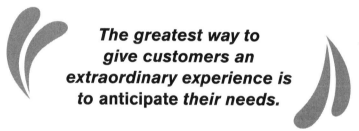

The greatest way to give customers an extraordinary experience is to anticipate their needs.

As a quick aside, FitBit is clearly in the Gather and Expand stages of SURGE. I wrote part of this chapter on a flight to Calgary. Once in the air, a flight attendant told me how much she loved her FitBit. When we landed, a couple came over to the outlets next to me to charge two FitBits. And without any prompting from me, they looked at me and said, "This thing is great." They went on for a few minutes, telling me why I need to get one and how great it is, not just in fitness but also in friendly competition. As I left to catch the next plane, the man yelled after me, "Hey... we don't work for FitBit." I know. I know. FitBit is just in the pocket.

If you have been following SURGE step by step, you will have a set of raving fans in short order. No question about it. This is because you first cherry-picked the group you will cater to in the Separate stage. You then aligned your offering to über-cater to their needs while staying true to your passion and purpose. And you have stirred them into a frenzy by rallying around a common mission, the Rally Cry. Now it's time to ride that wave for all it's worth.

STAY IN THE POCKET

In the Unify chapter, I told you about how David Schnurman built Lawline from a company with barely any clients and ten thousand dollars in annual revenue to the leading provider of continuing education for attorneys and five million in annual revenue. If you recall, David had figured out how to unify his offering, not just for the attorneys who took Lawline's courses, but also for the attorneys who *taught* the courses. Providing a platform for the attorneys to gain more exposure enabled him to attract more teachers, who spread the word about Lawline. Those teachers provided excellent content for attorneys taking their courses, who in turn also spread the word about Lawline. They shouted Lawline's Rally Cry, and the momentum carries Lawline forward to this day.

Once up on the wave, David became a master gatherer. He set up a system to get constant feedback from his customers and invited feedback on all of his courses. Out of the thousand-plus attorneys taking Lawline's courses every day, at least one hundred send in comments, about ten percent. The positive comments feed the company's purpose, constantly reminding the team *why* they are in business. The negative feedback brings about new solutions that keep Lawline in the pocket of the wave.

For example, Lawline introduced live broadcasts because they received critical feedback from consumers who wanted to be more engaged with the faculty. They wanted to be able to ask questions and interact with teachers. The result is a radically improved product that helps Lawline keep its momentum.

Alan Schnurman, David's father, told me that "David is an inspiration to all he comes in contact with. His mother and I included."

Agreed, Alan! David is a pretty badass surfer.

TINKER AND TWEAK

Chef Dominique Ansel knows all about the importance of the Gather phase. He knows that success happens when total preparation meets surging opportunity. Named one of the Top Ten Pastry Chefs in the United States in 2009, Ansel struck out on his own to join the growing trend of New York City confectioneries in 2011, opening his own unique bakery in SoHo. Because of his pedigree and his signature French selections, Ansel instantly made a name for himself on the New York trend scene, winning *Time Out New York's* "Best New Bakery" of 2012 within his first four months of business.

Ansel spent every spare moment experimenting. He was constantly tinkering with new combinations and ideas, looking for that signature item that would set his bakery apart from the crowd. He knew the essence of beating the competition was not in being better. Remember, from the customer's perspective, better is not better. *Different is better.*

Ansel was seeking something to make his bakery a destination not just for New Yorkers, but also for anyone looking for a truly unique dessert. His relentless tinkering led the *New York Post* to call Ansel "The Willy Wonka of NYC." His tempting pastry experiments, complemented with the steady stream of industry-insider accolades, rallied a small, faithful group of recurring customers who visited his bakery to sample all his latest concoctions. Ansel had identified the pocket of his wave, and continuously gathered knowledge from customers. If customers sampled something and then immediately bought more, he was onto something. If they didn't want more or didn't come back for more, the answer was obvious. Simple, but extremely effective data-gathering. Remember, customers speak the truth through their wallets. He had some minor hits, but Ansel wanted to find the pocket of the wave. In May of 2013, his tinkering led him to something he thought might really launch his bakery to another level. But even Willy Wonka himself couldn't have predicted just how big the core of this wave was going to be.

Ansel came up with a recipe for croissant pastry that would hold together in a deep fryer. Of course, everybody knows that if you deep-fry something it's going to be *way* tasty, but croissant dough doesn't traditionally hold up well in the fryer. Unfazed, Ansel perfected his recipe and then turned it into something really wicked, filling it full of vanilla cream. His new invention was flaky like a croissant, but shaped like a donut, filled with vanilla cream, and finished with a rose glaze and a light dusting of white powdered sugar. Flaky softness on the inside like a croissant, fried, sweet and sugary on the outside like a donut, and heaven throughout. Ansel had given birth to the one-and-only Cronut®. Take that, Wonka.

Ansel didn't expect much demand above his other creations, but the day's batch of Cronuts disappeared in a matter of minutes. When he opened the next day, a line of a couple dozen people had already gathered outside. The day's Cronut batch disappeared again shortly after people entered the bakery. Day three, and Ansel went to his door to find more than a hundred people already standing in line for—spoiler alert—Cronuts.

Within a few weeks, local network television affiliates had picked up the unlikely story: New Yorkers had gone "Cronut crazy," and Ansel was riding atop a wave that he couldn't have imagined or controlled. Cronuts were selling on the "black market" for hundreds of dollars. *Time* Magazine named the Cronut one of its "Top 25 Inventions of 2013." Every bakery quickly began trying to copy Ansel's creation, and there was a fight at the U.S. Patent office to grab the Cronut trademark. (Ansel ultimately won it.)

Being at the top of a wave of this size, it would have been easy for Ansel to suffer a major wipeout, but the time he invested in understanding the wave's pocket has enabled him to carve up the wave, leaving nothing but powder—the white sugar type—in his wake.

STAY FOCUSED ON YOUR NICHE AND UNIQUE OFFERING

How did a humble Cronut chef manage to hang ten on the custom pastry mash-up tsunami? He gathered his talents, aligned them with his faithful customers' core values, and from the time he first opened his bakery he zeroed in on one thing: finding the wave's pocket. Ansel focused on *the customer experience*. Ansel knew people weren't buying *food* when they went to a local eatery. They were buying an *experience*, and that was a wave Ansel had prepared his staff for from day one. Even today, riding high on a continuing wave of Cronut fever, Ansel realizes that his customers, waiting in line outside his bakery, are still the most important thing. On cold days, his staff passes out hot chocolate and hand warmers to the hundred or so people waiting for the doors to open.

And instead of changing that experience—several customers have said that waiting in line is part of what makes a Cronut so special—Ansel still limits the number of Cronuts he makes every day, and still offers new things on his menu on a regular basis. Ansel could have started serving nothing but Cronuts, opened extra kitchens and began producing that deep-fried flaky goodness twenty-four hours a day. But Ansel knew that wasn't what his customers were buying. The pocket of the wave was made evident by what his customers did and said. They flew in from all over the world for this experience. They made his bakery a special stop on tours of New York City. Ansel's pocket is delivering a limited quantity of unique, scarce pastry delights, not mass-produced crap. His customers want the same special confection they have come to expect from his bakery—or from what they've heard about his bakery—confections made even more special by their limited availability.

The pocket isn't just who you are serving. It is the what, why, when, where, and how. You need to constantly tweak the dials on all those elements to make sure your customers (the who) are consistently thrilled. For the Cronut, the who are people seeking those unique, scarce pastry delights. But there is more. They want a story to tell when they see their friends—so Ansel caters to them as they wait in line. The "what" is pushing the limits of

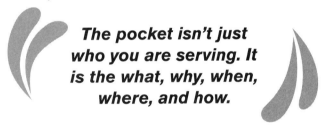

> **The pocket isn't just who you are serving. It is the what, why, when, where, and how.**

baking. The "where" is a small, almost back-alley part of New York City; it is only fitting for the most famous pastry to be made in the most famous city in the world. And of course the "why" is so that people can experience a little bit of heaven and wonderment, for real, right here on earth and in a New York bakery, of all places.

While your version of success might not resemble the Cronut craziness that Ansel saw, his Cronut story exemplifies what can happen when you know where the wave's pocket is and have the discipline to *only* ride there. The Gather phase is not passive. You are actively providing your service or product while simultaneously learning and tweaking. It is the rule of being in the right place, at the right time, on hyperspeed.

GATHERING 101

How do you gather information about your customers? You ask and you track. Ask and track. Ask and track. Say that five times really fast!

Look, my friends and close business associates—you know, the guys who kick my ass on Man Days—know that I am a bit obsessed with developing metrics and tracking progress. I realize I'm an oddball; you may not want to get as detailed as I get when I test new products or services, or track existing offerings. Still, you're going to have to learn how to gather and, at the very least, provide a system for someone *else* to track the information as a good geek would.

Start by interviewing your clients, or just asking them. Yes, I know, we're interviewing clients a lot. But you know what? They love it. They want the attention. They want to feel special. And if you don't ask, you'll never gain the information you need to stay in the pocket of your beautiful wave. A sit-down or phone interview is not always required. Like Chef Ansel, just ask customers specific questions when you have a chance. Do they like the new packaging? Are the hours convenient? Do they miss any of your discontinued products or services?

Next, add this task to your weekly schedule: "Be a fly on the wall." Read reviews of your products or services in the comment section of your website, as David Schnurman does with his daily digest of consumer comments. Read the comments and reviews of your offerings on third-party sites, in discussion forums, and in other places where your clients hang out. Make note of the commonalities. Keep track of the positive comments to bolster you and your team on rainy days, and use the negative comments as inspiration for tweaking your offering.

Test a new product or service by introducing it to just a few of your customers. Watch their behavior. Notice patterns. Keep track! Ultimately, the best way to measure the success of your offering is to watch people's behavior. Action is the ultimate truth.

Since I'm guessing you're not the tracking and systems geek I am, I have created handy-dandy spreadsheets for you to make gathering a snap. Visit www.MikeMichalowicz.com/resources to download these glorious spreadsheets. Some may call gathering tedious, but for me, it's more fun than Disneyland.

MAKING A PLAN TO RIDE THE WAVE

What would happen to your business if you found the pocket of your wave and suddenly experienced Cronut-level success? Would you be able to meet the demand? You need a plan and you might as well learn how to create one from the experts.

Do you have a plan in place to scale quickly? (That's what *The Pumpkin Plan* is all about.) How are you going to ensure profitability? (That's in *Profit First*.) What will you do if you are buried by an unplanned demand for your products or services? (Check out *Lean Startup* by Eric Reis for more on that). Need to have a sales guy who can sell ten times as much? (Dig into *Hyper Sales Growth* by Jack Daly.) How about your entire company selling *ten times* the volume you do today? (Read *Built to Sell* by John Warrillow… ten times.) What systems would need to be in place to do that? (I suggest *Traction* by Gino Wickman, and be sure to read *The E-Myth* by Michael Gerber. By all that is holy, read *The E-Myth*.) What type of people would you need? (Grab *Topgrading* by Geoff Smart.) How will you keep them pushing forward during the exciting but trying times? (Read *The Commitment Engine* by John Jantsch and *Start with Why* by Simon Sinek.) What resources would you need to have available and which ones can you get by without? (May I suggest *The Toilet Paper Entrepreneur*?) Limiting output is certainly one answer, as Ansel has used to his advantage. Or you may have only one shot at milking this cash cow for all it's worth and you need to move fast. (Seth Godin shares this in *Purple Cow.*) Regardless, the key is this: You need to start treating your business like a manufacturer and streamline it. (In addition to other projects, I am also working on *Streamline*, one of the three books in my "Sweet Spot" series. I know. I'm crazy. But I'm crazy for *you*.)

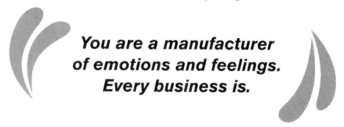

> **You are a manufacturer of emotions and feelings. Every business is.**

Even if you don't make a physical product, even if you are "just" a service provider, you are a manufacturer. I propose that *all* businesses are manufacturers. Yours included. Every business generates a final feeling or emotion for its customer. Every business goes through a sequence of events that results in that final emotion or feeling. You are a manufacturer of emotions and feelings. Every business is.

Maybe you are an accountant. In your case, you may be manufacturing a feeling of financial confidence. Maybe you have a transportation business. In your case, you are creating a feeling of safety, or perhaps efficiency. Maybe you are an author, which, as everyone knows, means you're kinda cool. In your case, you may be building a sense of confidence or clarity in your readers. No matter what it is, you are manufacturing; you are creating or building something.

Just like the grand old masters of manufacturing will tell you, two things bring about manufacturing perfection. First, reverse-engineer what you deliver. Start with the end prototype and then work backward on the process to create it consistently. So, if you manufacture financial confidence, reverse-engineer the exact steps that will deliver that confidence to your customers *every time*. If you generate a sense of safety, reverse-engineer that feeling. The point is this: To ride the wave of customer demand you must provide them with the right solution at the right time, and present it in the right way. It's all about consistency, people. Consistency! And that is exactly what you will achieve when you start operating your business like the manufacturer it truly is.

The second lesson from manufacturers is this: Reduce variability. The fewer steps you need to deliver your offering, the easier it is to be consistent and the more you can perfect each step. Fewer steps translate into higher quality deliverables with less effort: a win for your clients and a win for you. At first blush it sounds crazy, but start seeking ways to do less for your clients. Do fewer things remarkably well and surfing will be a breeze.

GET YOUR EARLY ADOPTERS PUMPED!

Paul Scheiter at Hedgehog Leatherworks, a manufacturer in which I have been an active investor for almost ten years now, has this down to a science. Over the years, Paul has developed a launch system for his products that leverages all the knowledge gleaned from the Gather phase. Paul received *Field & Stream*'s "2013 Product of the Year" award, and his now-famous Blackbird SK-5 Advanced Sheath is featured in the crescendo moment of every single episode of the Weather Channel's *Fat Guys in The Woods*. Paul walks hand in hand with the vendors who serve the survival and bushcraft industry: knife designers, axe makers, survival authors, survival experts. The list goes on and on.

Paul does one thing that keeps him tight in the pocket of the marketplace wave as it grows: he employs *exclusivity*, just like the Cronut guy. Just as you should.

When Paul considers expanding the Hedgehog Leatherworks product line, he contacts his most loyal customers. He tells them about his idea and gauges interest. If it is significant, he starts to share development sketches and pictures on a private section of his website. The product will not yet be available for purchase, but more feedback is gathered and the anticipation builds.

Then the day comes when a limited launch is announced, and the product is made available only to the loyal customers who participated in the gathering phase. Doors open, and sales often *flood* in. Why wouldn't these people want to buy? They got on an exclusive list to wait for just this opportunity, and they gave input on what they wanted most. Paul not only observes what his niche wants, he gathers direct feedback from

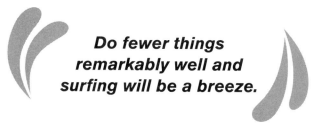

Do fewer things remarkably well and surfing will be a breeze.

them. Wouldn't you want access to something you helped create, even in part? That is the power of gathering knowledge and feedback from your community. Your separated community is separated from other markets, but they surely aren't separated from you. Not in the least. The niche becomes a co-creator. And who wouldn't want access to a product or service that few others have, and you helped create?

Once orders are no longer being accepted from this exclusive group, often after a few days, the products ship and customers finally get their hands on what they've been waiting for all this time. This is where the next Gather level happens. Paul measures the strength of the wave's pocket with a simple method of gauging interest. As his best clients start sporting their new Hedgehog Leatherworks product, Paul sees how much new demand begins to build up.

Paul measures how many email inquiries come in from people asking if the product will become available in the future. He tracks calls. He even tracks—and yes, this happens a lot—how many of the customers who just bought the exclusive sheath plead with him to make "just one more for my friend."

It is somewhat ironic that limiting the availability of your offering to the wave in the beginning is a perfect way to measure how well you are positioned in the pocket. Sometimes Paul gets buried in pleading emails and calls. Other times he doesn't. Either way, the knowledge he gathers is of the utmost value. When the phone rings off the hook, he knows he is in the pocket. When the phone is so quiet he wonders if the phone service has been cut off, he knows he is out of the pocket, and if he stays there too long his ride is over. So he goes with another limited sample product and tests the market again.

There is one additional, sweet surfing move Paul does. Just like any entrepreneur who loves his customers, sometimes he leaves the product as a special treat only available for his core following. Even if people beg and plead for a full public release of the product, that one sale is the only one that will ever happen. Consistency is a wonderful and necessary thing, but when everything is predictable, anticipation goes away. No one anticipates the amazingness of a Dunkin' Donuts donut as they do one of Chef Ansel's delicacies. That's why Paul, every so often and when you least expect it, rewards the exclusive group who bought a sheath during the gathering stage with a one-of-a-kind, never to be made again, gem of a product.

When my business partner, Ron Saharyan, and I decided to launch Profit First Professionals, Ron guided us through a similar process of limiting availability and quickly gathering insights. As we contemplated the offering suite for our initial launch, we began to tell our potential customer base that we were limiting our initial membership to only eight firms. While this scarcity certainly helped build the initial excitement about our program, we did it for another, more significant reason as well. Unlike Hedgehog Leatherworks, we didn't have established sales or an active customer base. So, in addition to creating an exclusive group of early adopters, we were also hoping that a small group of initial clients would help us to gather some much-needed feedback on our first products and services. The small number would make it possible for us to stay in close contact with our initial members and quickly make adjustments as we moved toward a much wider rollout.

Ron nailed it. Not only were we able to get eight initial clients to open Profit First Professionals, we actually had fifty accounting professionals who wanted in on the initial eight spots. We had managed to not only meet our initial goal, but also to gather a bit of Hedgehog's famed pre-launch exclusivity that would help us launch bigger in the next round.

But the real juice was in what we gathered. Soon after our inaugural membership joined, we were interviewing them. We adjusted our offering dynamically, killing off the stuff our members didn't care about and greatly improving what they did respond to. We were in *constant* contact with our early adopters, gathering, learning, and adjusting. Then it happened: Calls came in from aspiring members, who wanted to get in because of the results the inaugural eight were experiencing. One prospective member did everything short of bribing us. (If a bribe can be considered "short of a bribe.")

I remember Bert Jacobs, the cofounder of Life is Good®, telling me this same story. For the longest time he and his partner were in the Gather stage. Bert and his partner (who is also his brother from the *same* mother) John Jacobs were selling T-shirts at local fairs and parades in Boston with little success. But they loved their work, so they kept at it. With each day's proceeds, they would buy a keg and host a party at their (low-rent) apartment. The walls were covered with Burt and John's sketches, cartoons, and all types of phrases and jokes. Guests would party the night away and write comments on the walls about the pictures. Burt and John were partying through the Gather phase, literally.

Then the fateful morning happened. Burt was "cleaning up" the apartment—kicking a beer-filled cereal bowl off the coffee table—when he noticed all the comments about one particular drawing. The image of the now-iconic Life is Good character, Jake, was circled and highlighted a hundred times more than any other thing in the apartment, with the saying "Life is good" scrawled below it. Time for a test.

Beer money was quickly diverted to buy as many T-shirts as possible, all featuring a drawing of Jake smiling away, dead center on the front of the shirt, with the words "Life is Good" below his face. The shirts flew off the shelves (if you can consider the folding table they were using shelves). Everyone bought them: bikers, grandmas, awkwardly dressed twins. And then, the magic moment happened: Kids began trying to *steal* them.

The shirt was so hot that kids (and, as the story goes, a shifty grandma or two) were willing to risk a run-in with the law to get their hands on it. Life is Good was on top of the wave, standing tall and ready to carve the wave like no one in the T-shirt industry ever had before.

An undeniable indicator that you have Gathered all the elements to ride the wave and have moved your board to the wave's pocket is when people start breaking the rules to get what you've got. For Profit First Professionals, it was potential customers who were willing to bribe us to get in. (I don't admit or deny that it worked.) For Life is Good, it was customers willing to steal their product. For Hedgehog Leatherworks, it was the customers who mailed in (and continue to mail in) checks along with notes that say something to the effect of, "I don't care what sheath you make next, even if I hate the knife it is made for. I just have to have a Hedgehog sheath." For Chef Ansel, it was a hundred people lined up hours and hours before the store opened to get their mitts on a Cronut—even going so far as to hire line-holders to keep their spots so they could run off to the restroom. That's when you know without a doubt that you are in the pocket.

FINDING YOUR POCKET

When we last left Brian Smith, he had finally nailed the surfing market with his UGG boots. The path was a long slog for him, because he was having difficulty spotting the pocket of the wave. Ironic, since he *is* a surfer. But this isn't really surfing, after all, and getting to the pocket of the SURGE is not easy for most entrepreneurs. When you get up on the wave, it's usually your very first time. But instead of enjoying that moment of just making it up on your board, you need to move to the pocket and cut and carve, immediately. Real surfers get dozens of attempts every day. You? Not so much.

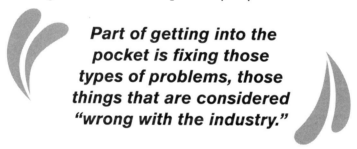

Part of getting into the pocket is fixing those types of problems, those things that are considered "wrong with the industry."

Avid surfers who devote their lives to surfing can easily surf five thousand waves in their lifetime. A typical entrepreneur, on the other hand, may choose to only surf *one* wave. Maybe two. The outlier may ride five to ten in a lifetime. An outlier of outliers may ride fifty. Think Richard Branson. So, as an entrepreneur, the first time you get up on a wave, you need to ride like a pro, because statistically this is going to be your one and only ride. But don't let "you only have one shot at the wave" intimidate you. The benefit in this comparison is that you have time—months, years, or in some cases a decade or two—to find the pocket, whereas the surfer only has a few seconds.

This was Brian's one and only wave and he struggled to find the pocket. But he kept looking. This is a lesson in itself; just because you can't find the pocket at first does not mean it's not there. Just keep looking.

Brian kept trying to sell his sheepskin boots to American surfers, but struggled to get traction. While the Aussie mates got it, the dudes in the States didn't. Again, the American consumer had a misconception of sheepskin, thinking it was like wool. That meant wet, soggy, and itchy. The boots looked bizarre. And they surely weren't cool.

Part of getting into the pocket is fixing those types of problems, those things that are considered "wrong with the industry." Ultimately, Brian cracked the code with the surfer market; then he created a growth formula that allowed him to rapidly expand into market after market using the cracked code. His expansion formula was simple:

1. The product needed to warm a community of people who had cold, damp feet and wanted to get them warm and dry without the need for socks. Brian's solution was the UGG boot itself, of course. It worked incredibly well, and the Australian consumer had proved it. He had a distinct, rock-solid product that catered to a specific, separated community: surfers.

2. To communicate with the American consumer, Brian could not use the term sheepskin, which equated with wool. Brian fixed this by using an industry term that most American consumers were not yet familiar with: shearling. Brian no longer needed to dispel the consumer's perception; the unfamiliar term gave him the benefit of the doubt.

Even though they were comfortable, the boots were bizarre-looking and no one in the surfing community would risk the potential of losing their cool factor by wearing such uncool boots. That is, of course, until Brian applied the solution: Get the coolest of cool pro and semi-pro surfers to wear the boots in advertisements and let them keep the boots as gifts. Wannabe cool people (which is pretty much everybody) feel compelled to emulate the *truly* cool people. Then as more wannabes copy the "be's," social pressure sets in, and more and more people comply. Brian's lesson? Gather the "cool kids."

WHAT IF YOU DON'T HAVE MANY (OR ANY) CUSTOMERS?

This one is simple. If you have just a few customers, then gathering information shouldn't take very long! Refer back to the Gathering 101 section earlier in this chapter and try to hit as many of the ideas as you can. If you don't have any customers yet, you have two options: You could take a pass on this step and wait until you do have customers, or you can gather information about feedback on your competitors' offerings using the same methods I shared in Gathering 101. Basically, either skip it or spy. If you have time on your hands, spying is fun. You may even get a few ideas that will help you refine your offer before you launch it. Just remember to keep track of your intel. No need to store it on a microchip or in a secret compartment, 'cause that is kinda creepy.

ACTION STEPS

1. Make a list of the people among your best clients who would jump at the chance to serve as early adopters of your new and/or improved offering.

2. Identify a service, product, or offering you can deliver to this exclusive group of your best customers for a short period of time. Measure their actions throughout the process. If you see them going to extreme measures to acquire your offering, you are in the pocket. If the interest is lukewarm, you're bobbing in the ocean. And the lukewarm feeling is probably because the guy bobbing next to you peed in your spot.

3. You might be near the pocket, but not spot on it. Make a list of high-level questions to ask your exclusive customers, to better discern if your product needs further tweaking or should be abandoned. Set plans in motion to adjust accordingly.

4. As you identify what is working, create a list of ways to simplify the delivery of your service or the creation of your product. You can only carve up a wave if you can deliver results with ease.

5. Download super helpful spreadsheets that will help you measure progress and track information at www. MikeMichalowicz.com/resources.

EXPAND

YOUR OBJECTIVE IN THIS FINAL STAGE OF SURGE IS CLEAR: Capture every ounce of energy from your wave and have it carry you as far as you can take your business. But if the objective seems simple, the method to achieve that goal is even more straightforward. To get everything you can from the Expand phase of the Surge, do more of what is working and less of what is not.

If you have a strong wave, you can surf it for many years or even countless decades (think Chuck Taylor All-Star sneakers). Sometimes the waves are strong but abrupt, and they may carry you for only a few years (think classic Crocs—you know, the shoes you wear to guarantee no one will ever date you). But no matter what, when you are in the wave's pocket, this is when you ride it for all it's worth. Surfers perform carves, cutbacks, turns, kick outs, aerials, lay backs, jumps, air reverses, and tons of monstrous shredding at this stage. You will do the same. In fact, you *must*.

You will know when you are in the pocket because customer demand for your offering continues to build on its own. This is the tipping point, as Malcolm Gladwell explained in his book called—ahem—*The Tipping Point*. This phase feels so easy because that big beautiful blue wave, the energy of the market, is pushing you forward. The desire may be to just stand up tall, cockily pursing your lips and half-nodding like Donald Trump while running your hand through your blondish, sea-breezed, combed-over hair. It is so easy to just stay still, look cool, and bask in all the staring from the beautiful people on the beach while the wave does all the work.

And that is exactly what you *can't* do, because suddenly you're ass-in-the-air, flying right over the nose of your board, and in another moment it will seem like the whole ocean just fell on top of you. In half a heartbeat, you're pushed down to the ocean floor

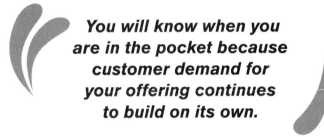

You will know when you are in the pocket because customer demand for your offering continues to build on its own.

and torn apart on the reef. One second you're standing on top of the wave, flaunting your genius, and the next second you're tombstoned. It happens that fast. In a snap, you can go from carving up seawater to sucking it down.

So, what happened?

One of two things. Either you thought your work was over (that's a big mistake), or you thought you should keep doing the same thing over and over (that's an even bigger mistake). Countless businesses die after having early success riding their SURGE. Things are going so well that they stagnate in the status quo. They stop improving; they stop pushing to expand their customer base. Instead, they stay exclusively focused on that initial core customer group from the Gather stage and never expand to serve the greater wave. They experience a small initial push, only to lose focus and let the wave leave them behind.

Once you have gotten yourself in the pocket, you transition to Expand to reap the rewards of your work. Now you do all you can to shred the wave, while the entire world watches (and buys!) in awe.

TWO FOR ONE

I have a little secret to tell you. Each of the first four stages of SURGE served two purposes. First, the obvious: they put you on top of the wave, making money and ready to scale, big time. The second purpose is not so obvious: It showed you exactly how you need to proceed going forward. It gave you your own custom, step-by-step growth formula. By learning the exact things that your best customers want and the exact way they want them, you now know exactly what you need to do to clone more markets. Or in surfing terms, the first four stages taught you how to shred.

Cloning markets that share similarities to your initial market may seem impossible, but you've already got the formula for success. Remember how you cloned your best *clients* by learning everything you could about them? You asked core questions, and, I hope, dozens more to learn about their industry. You investigated and qualified their niche. You studied and talked with industry experts. And most importantly, you continue to closely observe those customers.

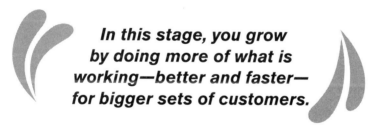

In this stage, you grow by doing more of what is working—better and faster— for bigger sets of customers.

Now it's time to Expand by cloning this initial market, replicating the specific elements that are working for your existing customer niche. You document the things that are working in your core market and replicate that process for a new market that is structured in the same way.

The Expand phase is the polar opposite of stagnation. In this stage, you grow by doing more of what is working—better and faster—for bigger sets of customers. Just like the OSI improved Steve Austin by making him bionic. Steve was already an awesome astronaut and test pilot, but scientists turned him into an even more awesome secret agent by amplifying what he was already able to do and making him better than he ever was: better, stronger, faster. I know it's not surfing, but come on! *The Six Million Dollar Man*, right? Anybody? Rudy? Jaime? Oscar? Anybody?

Perhaps another lesson from Brian Smith would help.

THE EXPANSION FORMULA

Once Brian Smith found the pocket of his wave, his UGG business saw explosive growth in the surfer community. He was now ready to take the first four stages of SURGE and develop an expansion formula. The new question was, "What other markets are clones of the surfer market?" In other words, *who* else: one, had cold, damp feet that needed to get warm? Two, didn't know what shearling was (and didn't care)? And three, had a community that copies the cool kids?

The obvious answers were other sporting communities that suffered from cold, damp feet. Track stars and football studs surely weren't a match—they had hot, sweaty feet. But hockey players and skiers were an obvious fit. So, Brian made a road trip to the mecca of US hockey: Canada.

In every Canadian town and in the big hockey states like Minnesota, Michigan, and Wisconsin, Brian had an opportunity. He got to work and followed his formula. Get the semi-pro hockey studs of the area to pose for ads wearing UGG boots. Then bammo, sales would launch. Next city, same formula. Bammo. Hockey players, skiers, even hunters, were all getting UGGs. Then Brian decided to go after the strongest, toughest, no-bullshit competitors of all time: teenage girls.

On a long flight back to California, Brian got stuck next to a teenage girl who was snapping her gum and flipping through celebrity mags like *People* and *Us Weekly*. As he looked around the cabin, he could see his seatmate wasn't the only one reading these magazines. Women of all ages pored over the pages of these chronicles of cool, looking at picture after picture of the famous and not-so-famous. The only thing that moved faster than the pages was the shift between snarky comments and oohs and aahs.

Brian realized that the young female, celebrity-emulating market was no different than the surfers, hockey players, skiers, and hunters who were already buying his boots. These women were watching what the cool kids, the celebrities, were wearing and then emulating them. Teenage girls were most ravenous for the latest Hollywood celebrity styles. Brooke Shields, Gwen Stefani, and Britney Spears (this is the early 2000s, mind you) made fashion trends cool overnight. One picture of Brooke Shields wearing a pair of UGG boots would get teenage girls to take notice. This market was no different than the others he was now in. No different at all, with one exception. It was ten thousand times bigger.

The formula was established: number one, warm feet with no socks; number two, funky-looking boots with a funky name; number three, market's "cool kid" wears them. Numbers one and two of the formula were taken care of. Now the question was, how to get a celebrity to wear them? Hiring Brooke Shields for a photo shoot was so far out of Brian's budget it wasn't even a consideration. But supplying free boots to Brooke Shields's stylist was doable.

Brian headed to Hollywood with a simple plan. Identify the top stylists for celebrities and give them free pairs of UGGs. The stylists were on the cutting edge of fashion and they had the undivided one-on-one attention of celebrities. Stylists were effectively a walking showroom of fashion. Celebrity stylists are trusted advisers who are responsible for everything their clients wear, from hair and makeup to clothes. The stylists are paid to be one step ahead of the celebrities themselves and to keep their clients looking good. Many fashion designers know the importance of having Hollywood stylists take a liking to your designs, and Brian had just dropped his lowly UGGs among the likes of Christian Dior and Calvin Klein in the dressing rooms of Tinseltown.

Fast forward to a frigid New York winter day, and the paparazzi snap a picture of none other than Brooke Shields, walking down the sidewalk wrapped in a warm winter coat and accessorized with a pair of tan UGG boots. Surf's up.

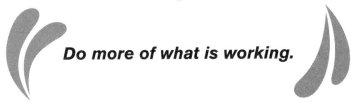

Do more of what is working.

Then the biggest influencer in the world made her declaration. In 2000, Oprah Winfrey herself featured UGG boots on "Oprah's Favorite Things," her annual Christmas gift show extravaganza. *Tidal wave.* The next day, sales exploded.

The Expand method is simple. Document the formula that worked for your primary niche market. Seek the other markets that are structured the same way and then repeat that formula in those markets. Do more of what is working. The method is easy. The execution is the hard part.

Profit First Professionals is not at the Expand stage yet. It is way too early. In order to expand, we need to be the authority in the market and we aren't there yet. We can consider expansion when we become a "household name" within our niche. And when we begin that discussion, we have to take the sellout risk into account. Do we want to replicate PFP for lawyers? Doctors? Musicians? If we expand, will we risk selling out the accountants and bookkeepers we serve now?

The Expand phase of SURGE is by far the longest part of the cycle, or at least I hope it is for you. Expanding is about being alert to the wave as it rolls forward and morphs. The pocket itself will change, and so will the elements around it. As you continue to ride your wave through the Expand phase, you'll be seeing all the small (or big) opportunities within the wave and move to take advantage of each one. The great part is that you no longer need to spot the wave or paddle to sync up with it. Now, it's about cutting and carving on all the best parts of your wave. It's about having the discipline to stay in control and focused on the important part of your wave as the surf crashes all around you.

SELL OUT

Oh lordy-lord it pains me to say this, but it's time. It's finally time. Def Leppard sucks.

If you agree, that means you are a Def Leppard purest, and you were likely part of the initial, surging wave pocket that pushed the band to its early success. Of course, if you disagree and think Def Leppard rocks, you are part of the greater wave (one that's definitely now in its final fading phase). And if you don't know what (or who) Def Leppard is and don't have one iota of curiousness, then you don't make up any of the wave. Just as in the ocean, where the vast majority of water is not part of, and never will be part of, the wave. The waves roll by and the rest of the water is just moved *through*. In your SURGE, the folks that make up your wave today won't be the same folks that make up your wave tomorrow, and some will never be a part of your wave at all.

My number one "desert island" album is Def Leppard's *Pyromania*. They were awesome—*then*. Yet Def Leppard has sucked ever since that album.

If you had known me back in the day, you would never have believed that I would one day be capable of saying such sacrilegious words. When I was in my pubescent-hormonal-rage year at the start of 1983, I was a hardcore Def Leppard fan. Then they sold out. I strongly suspect that you have your own version of a "they sold out" story. Undoubtedly there was a band or musician that *you* went gaga over. And then, one day, you realized that they don't give a *crap* about you. You realized that everything cool they did, all those things that spoke to you, that connected with you, and their Rally Cry that you shouted from every rooftop in town, had been abandoned. Either you outgrew them or, more likely, they outgrew you.

Perhaps you're familiar with the adhesive called Gorilla Glue. What you may *not* know is, Gorilla Glue was first used by Indonesian furniture makers to assemble teak furniture. Then Gorilla Glue used their super-strong bonding formula to expand to general consumers, who need to fix a sticky situation with stickiness. Now Gorilla is into everything from tape to self-standing bags. Gorilla *expanded*, but to the folks who run Bagoes Teak, Gorilla is surely a sellout. To Jimmy's mom, who just wants to glue together the collapsing shoe box/school project Jimmy made so she can go to bed sometime this decade, Gorilla Glue is a godsend. The same is true for anyone needing to make a quick fix. Gorilla Glue's massive success in the past decade has been due, in no small part, to moving on from Indonesian furniture makers.

Back to Leppard. Every generation has its wave of teenage energy and rage, and for me that wave hit in 1983 (if you count shooting spitballs at the back of your friends' heads as rage). The cool kids at school were listening to Def Leppard, so I rushed out to Sam Goody in the spring of 1983 on my banana-seat bike (it used to have tassels on the handlebars, but I ripped them off... in a fit of rage) and bought the first cassette I ever owned—*Pyromania*.

Every teenager who was cool—or wanted to *feel* cool—bought *Pyromania*. Def Leppard was up on the wave, riding the pocket and getting ready to carve, with a relentless surge of acne-ridden fans pushing them forward. I bought all their albums: *High N' Dry*, *On Through The Night*, and a long-since backlisted EP, *Ride Into the Sun*. I played my cassettes until they were so worn my cassette player ate them. Then I hopped on the old banana-seat bicycle and bought replacements. I couldn't wait for their next album, which was the first big carve Leppard made on their wave.

With the release of *Hysteria*, Def Leppard entered a bigger market. Their target was the Top 40… you know, like Britney Spears, but with even tighter pants and way more hairspray. As far as I was concerned, Leppard was no longer speaking to teenage boys like me as much as they were speaking to moms who wanted to revisit their teenage years. The band had moved on to the one-step-away-from-easy-listening wave; the type of music that KMart would proudly sell during "Blue Light Specials." Def Leppard became a ballad production machine. Def Leppard sold out.

The number one hit on *Hysteria* was "Love Bites," and that's when the initial wave of teens started chanting, "Leppard Bites." The initial rise in the wave was collapsing, and Def Leppard smartly, albeit to my chagrin, moved to a bigger, better part of the wave.

You will need to do the same. You will need to be a sellout. It is inevitable. If you only ride the energy of that initial market, you'll find your ride over quickly—unless the market's interest stays constant (it rarely does), its consumers never change how they spend money (that almost never happens), or they never get older or die (unfortunately, that has a pretty poor track record).

When Brian Smith expanded into mass-market fashion, surfers jumped off the UGG wave (lame pun totally intended). Ask any cool surfer about UGGs today; they won't be caught dead wearing a pair. Yet UGGs are so pervasive in the fashion market that more than one quarter of American women own a pair. It's ironic. UGG was labeled as a sellout by surfers, but it was surfers who abandoned UGG. UGG still had the perfect solution for surfers, but since UGG now marketed their product to non-surfers, surfers felt abandoned. So they labeled UGG as a "sellout" and kissed UGG goodbye.

When Def Leppard expanded into the pop music market, metal fans went to Metallica. When Paul Orfalea, the founder of copy chain Kinko's—subsequently purchased by FedEx—abandoned college campuses to occupy all the strip malls in America, college students abandoned Kinko's to get their theses copied by other local shops. Facebook rode the wave of college campuses too, before selling out to every mom—and most of the dads—on the planet. Then college students went running from Facebook. Google was heralded by the Internet nerd do-no-evil wave, and now is labeled "evil" by that very crowd as Google finds new ways to monetize their stranglehold on search.

 **Your initial market will only take you so far.**

There is one guarantee: Whatever part of the wave you are riding right now, it is going to crumble. Expanding your business necessitates the crumbling of the initial market, and vice versa. You can't serve two masters, after all. When you expand, your initial market will crumble too. To your early fans, you will be a sellout. They will feel you abandoned them to move to bigger markets. And they are right. It may be a tough time emotionally, but it is the only way you can keep riding the wave. Your initial market will only take you so far. If you stick with your initial market for the distance, at a certain point, the wave will fold over or just peter out. Your ride will be over, and you will need to start from scratch. To keep your momentum, you *must* always keep moving to the newest, strongest part of the wave.

As soon as you find the formula that works for your initial market and the market is carrying you, you need to spend every waking moment catering to it, and every sleeping moment dreaming about what other markets will be served by the same formula. You need to actively find a new part of the wave to ride. You need to prepare to be a sellout.

...UNLESS YOU'RE LEGO

Exceptions exist for every rule. Heck, I feel *I'm* usually the exception to the rule (and I hope you feel that way too). I built my businesses by breaking rules and ditching conventional ideology. This is how I express my badassery. Badassedness. Badassity... you get my drift.

If there is one company that defies my theory that all waves crumble eventually, it's LEGO. The Lego Group, founded in Denmark in 1932 by Ole Kirk Christiansen, has been riding the same wave for decades. Though they have tweaked their products over the years, it's still basically the same concept—interlocking bricks and other parts that connect and provide kids (and adults) with endless hours of creative play. A multibillion-dollar company, The Lego Group competes with thousands of toy companies that offer thousands of different kinds of toys, and yet they're still killing it. So much so that in February of 2015, LEGO replaced Ferrari as Brand Finance's "world's most powerful brand."

Prepare to be a sellout. But maybe, just maybe, you'll be LEGO.

WHAT IF YOU DON'T HAVE MANY
(OR ANY) CUSTOMERS?

Okay. I want you to sit down for second. Well, since you're reading this book, you're probably already sitting. Unless you're walking the treadmill and listening to this on audiobook. (Shout out to all audiobook lovahs!) Wherever you are, I want you get real close to me and just listen for a second. I suspect that, at least to some degree, you can't imagine ever being a sellout. I mean, who would want to be? You have probably criticized others for being sellouts just as I have.

But here's the dealio, just as with everything else in Surge: What got you here won't get you there. The unique thing that you did to cater to your special niche market is the very thing the larger community doesn't want. More people like Top 40 music than 1980s hair band music. More people like vanilla ice cream than pistachio. It's the ultimate irony, but that thing that made you so unique and different and appealed to your niche is the same thing that's too edgy and different for the broader market.

You don't have to be a sellout, but you will have to make the tradeoff.

Now, lean in closer. Let me put my arm over your shoulder and whisper something in your ear. You don't have to be a sellout, but you will have to make the tradeoff. Do you want to continue to cater exclusively to your niche and live on in folklore, like Johnny Appleseed? Or do you want to take your business all the way to the beach and become an industry-defining organization, the next Google of your field?

Neither choice is wrong. Strike that—a choice is only wrong if you ignore what your soul calls out to do. Think about that for a bit. Take a drink of apple cider (wink), and go with your heart.

ACTION STEPS

1. Define the unique needs you are serving for your current market. Then make a list of "clone" markets to which you could expand.

2. Now brainstorm ideas for reaching that market. Who are the key influencers in that market—the "cool kids"—and how can you get their attention?

3. Start a document and title it "GOING MAINSTREAM." Jot down notes about what you'll have to do to prepare your company to sell out. Will you have to systematize even more aspects of your business? Will you have to stop catering to your original niche? What can you do to still show your original fans that you love them?

WIPEOUT! 8

THE POWER OF THE SURGE IS AN AMAZING THING. IT IS A massive force that will push your business forward to a degree you could never have fathomed on your own. When you catch the SURGE, your job is not to put effort into moving forward through your own movement alone; instead, your effort transitions to channeling the natural force behind you to *power* you forward. You switch from exerting tons of energy to using a much subtler, fluid technique of balance, observation, and direction. If you follow the SURGE steps, you have a real shot at catching that ideal wave and riding it all the way to the bank.

But just like everything else in life, nothing's perfect—except for my wife (guess who's going to get lucky tonight), Mom's homemade Mile High apple pie, and Def Leppard (before they became cheesy sellouts). Welcome to the caveat chapter, my friend.

You see, it's not all blue sky and beach babes here at the seashore. Like any seasoned surfer, you'd better know all about the problems you can run into when you end up on the wrong side of a wave, or when rough conditions make it better to stay onshore than to head out toward stormy waves in the dark of night. Vision is the key to surfing, both in the ocean and in business, as you ride your wave.

You have no control over the marketplace wave, whether good or bad, big or small, unpredictable or obvious. Just like a surfer, you have absolutely no control over the wave itself, only how you stand on it. You must master the techniques of capturing and leveraging the energy of the marketplace wave, but not try to control it.

Even the biggest surfers in the world, like Coca-Cola and Harley-Davidson, can't control the wave. That doesn't mean they haven't tried. The abject failures of New Coke, "Legendary" (not!) Harley-Davidson perfume, and McDonald's attempt to class things up a little with the Arch Deluxe all point to how crushing marketplace waves are when a company ignores its natural path and tries to direct or create waves on its own.

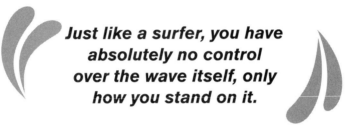

Just like a surfer, you have absolutely no control over the wave itself, only how you stand on it.

A wrong move during your SURGE can kill your business. But don't fret. This chapter is your lifeguard. Can you see him running down the beach toward you with the red float in one hand, whistle in the other? He looks a bit like David Hasselhoff in his finest days: handsome, buff, and sober. Who is that muscular stud?! So hard to make out that chiseled face in the bright glow of his perfect white teeth. Hold on. Now I can see him. Can you? OMG! *It's me.*

In Dale Carnegie's must-read book, *How to Stop Worrying and Start Living* (seriously, if you have not read that book yet, get it *immediately*), he shares a powerful strategy for navigating both life's biggest challenges and its biggest opportunities. "First ask yourself: What is the worst that can happen? Then prepare to accept it. Then proceed to improve on the worst."

The bonus to preparing for the worst-case scenario is that you can put containment measures in place to lessen the damage. By preparing—even if your new initiative knocks you off the wave—the damage can be contained and you can afford yourself time to paddle out to the next wave that comes along. Successful SURGErs know that all businesses are fraught with the possibility of failure;

the key is to fail *fast*, fail *small*, and *quarantine* the failure from affecting anything else. Like a nuclear power plant.

Because failure of a nuclear power plant could mean massive destruction and death, engineers put a lot of thought into how to fail safely. This came into the world news once again on March 11, 2011, when a 9.0 earthquake hit Japan, followed forty-one minutes later by a giant tsunami, and then another just eight minutes later. This was devastation far beyond what anyone could have imagined the six reactors at Fukushima Daiichi would be subjected to, but its engineers had planned for disaster.

While the magnitude of the earthquake's power was unimaginable—it literally shifted the Earth's axis and thus shortened the length of a day by roughly one microsecond—and the destruction was unspeakable, not one person died due to reactor explosions or radiation sickness. Though Japan received much criticism for its supposed "lack of preparedness," the country did a pretty remarkable job at controlling the nuclear calamity.

Contrast the planning in Japan with the complete lack of safety systems in Russia's Chernobyl nuclear power plant disaster in 1986, in which at least forty-one people died due to the explosions and resulting radiation sickness. While Japan has started putting nuclear reactors back on line recently, the Chernobyl city, Pripyat, devastated in April of 1986, stands today in ruins while the government, nearly thirty years later, is still trying to contain escaping radiation by building a massive barrier over the original sarcophagus structure that failed to contain the escaping radiation in the first place.

Of course your wrong move won't have the dire consequences of a nuclear accident, but its effects on your business (and you personally) could certainly be devastating and enduring if you don't find ways to properly limit your exposure to risk before you start. It's better to plan your exit hatches before a failure actually happens than to try to figure things out in the heat of the moment.

Now it's time to learn how to spot the early indicators of a potential earthquake, tsunami, or anything else that could trigger a nuclear meltdown in your SURGE plans, and what to do about it… Hasselhoff style.

GET REAL

Recently, I took a crack-o'-dawn call from an excited (yet notably drained) early-stage business owner. For the first few years his company had made less than one hundred thousand in annual revenue, but this call was his "SURGE." (Note… I put "SURGE" in big-time air quotes).

The previous morning, he had written three thousand dollars of business, and he was incredibly excited. "I did the math, Mike," he told me. "Three thousand bucks of business every day is a million-dollar business! I just did three grand in one day, and delivered everything… with a little help from my family and a few friends. Now I know what it's like to run a million-dollar company! I'm ready!"

An exciting day for sure. Something that I congratulated him for profusely. But also a SURGE red flag.

"You're *not* ready," I said. While he had every reason to be excited about his big order, he didn't know anything about running a million-dollar company. I explained to him, "You had family members and friends help you fill the order. You worked through the night to get it done. You had to call in favors and work to the point of exhaustion to pull it off. You did it for one day, but can you do that every day? That's what a million-dollar company does, and you aren't ready for that."

After celebrating the big order, what he needed to do was understand that this should actually be a wake-up call. If he did get that many orders every day, he'd be crushed under his wave instantly because he hadn't thought out how to grow quickly enough to manage that much business. What looked like a dream come true could easily turn into a nightmare, if he wasn't prepared for it.

Did you ever see that UPS commercial from years ago about the little startup company that launches and experiences a surge? In the opening scene, ten or so employees of "VertaBiz.com" quickly gather around the company's lead web developer as he counts down in front of his computer. "Three. Two. One." And he says, "We are officially open for business." There is a look of stressful anticipation in everyone's eyes. A close-up, funny shot shows an employee breathing out of a crumpled paper lunch bag to keep from hyperventilating. A close-up of the computer screen shows an "Orders Taken:" field that hangs at 0.

Then, after what feels like an eternal wait, the first order finally arrives. "Orders Taken: 1." You see a distant shot of all the employees sighing in relief. Then the orders jump to 35. More relief. Another employee rips the paper lunch bag out of the (no longer) stressed guy's hands. More orders come pouring in. "Orders Taken: 474." Cheers. High-fives. "Orders Taken: 2,095." Pure jubilation. Then, the turning point…

"Orders Taken" surges to 73,498… and keeps scrolling beyond 126,000. Silence. Panicked faces appear. The lunch bag-breather swallows uncomfortably. Orders skyrocket past 358,000. The lead computer guy is going to throw up. That is when the UPS announcer comes on and says, "Facing a virtual reality?"

Brown paper lunch bag, breathing in and out again.

Surfing without preparation kills you.

Pop!

BEWARE THE MINORITY OF THE MINORITY

The very nature of SURGE means listening to the minority, a segment of a market. Brian Smith was talking to the California surfer. Chef Dominique Ansel was connecting with the foodie—more specifically, the unusual dessert foodie. You, too, are talking with a very specific community.

Beware, because in that community will be impostors. Brian Smith surely had surfers from all over the world testing out the California waves. Some of those folks called Southern Florida, or Central America, or another area with a year-round warm climate, home. They are surfers, all right. Surfer fashion matters to them, but they don't have to face the problem of ice-cold feet. If Brian had listened to their feedback on UGGs, it would have taken him down the wrong path. Feedback from the minority outsiders that are hanging out with the minority insiders you are targeting can distract you so much that you lose focus on the wave and wipe out.

All feedback is not the same. As you gather thoughts, reviews, and insights from your community, qualify the people giving the feedback. If they are not your *exact* target, give a lot less credence to their feedback. I am sure that makes sense to you logically, but emotionally it is another game altogether.

Think about Chef Ansel. He is not a baker; he is an artist. Each Cronut® is a piece of art. Ninety-five percent of the foodies who eat it *love* it. Three percent are neutral. And two percent are impostors. That two percent, if he listens to them, will throw him off his game. That two percent may be barking about the ridiculous amount of calories in the Cronut, even though it is obviously the antithesis of healthy food. They may slam the odd texture. They may freak over the stickiness of the glaze.

A quick scan of Yelp will identify these haters. Of the 1527 reviews up on the morning that I checked, 1128 were four- or five-star, and 71 were one-star. If the product is consistent (which it is), how can there be such volatility? Because different groups of people are trying Cronuts. Most are equivalent to the Californian surfers—the right target audience, with the pain that can be fixed. Some are equivalent to the Floridian surfers—impostors, without the pain that the product can fix. And some are not even close, total impostors—for instance, someone standing on the beach who carries the dual curse of thalassophobia and pica. Not only do they fear entering the ocean, they have a disorder that makes them want to eat crazy things, like clothing—like UGG boots—and that review just *can't* be good.

A two-star review from Linnea E. says, "So I finally got my Cronut. Wow, what a letdown. They really aren't even good. Waaaayyyyy too much filling. One bite and it goes oozing everywhere. The [pastry] itself tastes like it was made a day or two in advance (it probably wasn't, but the point is, they don't taste fresh). Texture is rather chewy. The thyme flavoring overpowered everything else."

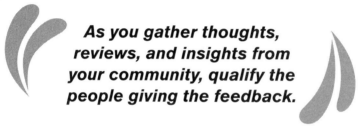

As you gather thoughts, reviews, and insights from your community, qualify the people giving the feedback.

The question that Chef Ansel must ask is, is she my Californian surfer? If the answer is yes, he needs to pay attention and ratchet down that thyme flavor. Is this a one-time problem or a recurring problem? If it is a one-time mistake, he needs to address the customer himself and make things right. If it is a recurring problem, he needs to address his business processes and make them right. But if she is not the Californian surfer (target market) equivalent, then he can't let her critical feedback sway him to move in any direction, because it is not relevant. Surely he should try to resolve her specific problem (perhaps by offering a refund), and also dissuade her from coming back (perhaps by giving her coupons to Dunkin' Donuts).

You will get complaints and negative reviews. These insights can be of tremendous value to your business, *if* you distinguish your minority from the impostors. If it is your target market giving a bad review, you must find a way to fix it for the individual and for the ongoing business process. If the one-star is from an impostor, you need to have the emotional fortitude to disregard the feedback and immediately put your attention back on your target market.

No one is immune to this. This book that you are reading right now will surely get five-stars, one-stars, and everything in between. My job is to evaluate which feedback is from my marketplace wave. If a fan of my other books has issues with this one, I need to fix that, big time. But if it is a fan of a traditional academic read—one of those historical, leather-bound, five hundred-page books stored in a secure section of the New York Library, which release a Harry Potter magic spell when the librarian blows the dust off—critiques this book, I need to have the emotional fortitude to disregard it and stay focused on my community.

Do the same.

BETTER IS NOT BETTER

It is easy to watch another business carve up the waves and simply say that you will copy what they do, but just do it better. It is easy to believe that when the marketplace sees you are better they will flock to you, but this is untrue. The moment you put your effort into being better than your competition is an early indicator that you are about to tank. Trying to be better means you are trying to catch a wave that has passed and are paddling uselessly, exhausting yourself. Trying to be different is how you paddle in front of a new wave; different gets noticed by the marketplace and gets you into position to be carried by it.

Energy is such a crucial commodity when it comes to starting a new business or launching a new product that you need to think about how to maintain that energy throughout the early part of the SURGE. An incredible amount of work goes into planning and initial product design, and then that energy shifts to maintaining constant contact with your early customers and providing the necessary shifts and tweaks to keep your business aligned with their needs and the momentum of the surge. If you fail to keep your energy levels balanced, you and your team could run low at the worst time imaginable, and the wave could just sweep past you.

Once that wave is gone, it's gone. Trying to paddle and catch up to a wave is impossible, and finding that momentum once you've lost it could be just as hard. The problem comes from the fact that your energy expenditure needs to ramp up exponentially as the wave passes you, because the wave is so much more powerful than you are alone. That's why you were trying to catch the wave in the first place—because you wanted to harness that power. Chasing it is nearly useless.

Your better bet is to cut your losses and begin paddling for the next wave. There are many waves out there, and it's not worth using up all of your energy and resources to chase the one that got away when you can use that same energy to get in position for the next. To keep from wasting your time and resources, it's important that you get off the wave as quickly as possible when you realize you've lost it.

KNOW YOUR LIMITS

Every company has limited energy. You also have limited resources and talent. Part of the effort involved in the Unify step of SURGE is in making sure you align your effort with the resources and people you have at hand, focusing your efforts on that one wave that is perfect for you. But too often, growing businesses try to surf waves they can't handle. Or worse, they dilute their efforts by trying to expand too quickly or take on multiple markets way too early. Part of knowing your limits is knowing *exactly* the wave you're going to surf and focusing all of your efforts there. You need to dominate your niche. Surf *your* wave.

One company you may not think of as having any limits is the global conglomerate that is today's Procter and Gamble; few people realize its humble beginnings. P&G was once a small company that had only two product lines—candles and soap. But instead of expanding into more lines to make the company grow, they actually focused it further by getting rid of their candle business so they could focus *only* on soap. Doesn't seem very sexy, does it?

That focus paid off in an odd way for P&G when they stumbled upon Ivory soap. Either by accident or design, depending on what legend you want to believe, sometime around the early 1900s, the folks at P&G found that they could extend the mixing time when making their popular Ivory soap bars and that this "whipping" of the soap introduced air bubbles into the bars, causing them to float. This "floating bar" became an important

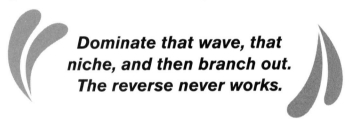

Dominate that wave, that niche, and then branch out. The reverse never works.

part of P&G catching its first big wave with America's entry into World War I. Before the first Great War, fighting had been pretty much a localized, daytime affair. In WWI, however, war became a far-flung, twenty-four-hour-a-day effort. Troops needed to bathe when and where they could, and the floating Ivory soap bar made that easy. Whether soldiers bathed in a large communal bath on board a troopship or in a stream, the Ivory soap with which they were equipped floated and stayed easy to find. This feature helped P&G dominate the military supply niche with their soap and helped them solidify their company to dominate in the consumer space as well.

This story is unique, but not unusual. History is filled with stories of companies that started out as niche players and became bigger after dominating that niche. Microsoft is gigantic today, but it started out focusing on one product: the Disc Operating System known as DOS. Apple focused development of the early Mac on the education market and dominated classrooms across the US before branching out to graphic design and the arts and then eventually going mainstream. You can be big, too. But first you need to pick a wave that you can ride with the resources you have at hand. Dominate that wave, that niche, and then branch out. The reverse never works.

KNOW WHEN TO DUMP YOUR WAVE

My last warning to you is to know when your wave is coming to an end. If you want to keep surfing, you know there comes a time that you must give up on your wave before it takes you so far into shore that you'll spend all of your energy just getting back out into the surf. Every wave runs out eventually. It's just a question of when. But so many companies don't get off the wave when they should, because once they've put in all the work needed to get up on that board they just hate the idea of losing all that easy momentum. Paddling for the next wave can seem a lot harder, but in the end it's easier to grab that next wave while you still have some momentum left from your current run.

One company that has seemed to have a great eye for when to change waves is Intuit. Initially finding the coming wave of personal finance software when the company began with Quicken back in 1983, it was able to use its head start to hold off a major assault from Microsoft's Money software in the early 1990s. When Intuit saw that many people were trying to keep their small business finances on Quicken—remember to always look for your customers trying to beat their own path, or breaking rules—they made a move to provide a small business accounting package, buying rights to an existing double-entry accounting package and reworking it into what would become QuickBooks. Today, QuickBooks dominates small business accounting on the desktop.

Around the same time Intuit provided its early small business accounting package to consumers, it also saw the possibility of tax preparation moving onto the personal computer, as well as the possibilities inherent in creating an easy bridge between personal accounting and tax preparation software. So, in 1993, Intuit purchased a San Diego company called ChipSoft and its flagship product, TurboTax.

Intuit could have ridden the waves of these three programs for a long time, but they could see new waves on the horizon that might dump them from their dominant position, and they continued to make moves to stay on top of the coming tides. The online software-as-a-service (SaaS) wave was bearing down on personal finance software, with services like Mint.com popping up to compete with Quicken. Free to use and easy to set up, Mint was set to topple Quicken's personal finance management dominance. Intuit could see that wave coming, and so, in 2009, Intuit simply purchased Mint.com, making the jump online and knocking out a tough competitor in one move. Intuit has now successfully moved all of its desktop software online, with SaaS versions of TurboTax and QuickBooks available in addition to their desktop counterparts—another carve of the wave getting Intuit back in the pocket. Only time will tell if the company can stay there.

To learn from a company that didn't know when to change waves, look no further than Blockbuster Video. An early powerhouse in home entertainment in the 1980s and '90s, Blockbuster failed to see that its wave was about to be done in by new, less expensive distribution channels. Netflix could deliver movies to customers less expensively through the mail, which negated Blockbuster's convenience advantage. After all, what's more convenient than having a movie delivered right to your door? And it was cheaper!

What Netflix didn't offer was the ability to pick up a movie the same day you wanted it, as you could do at Blockbuster. But Blockbuster lost that advantage, too, when Coinstar, Inc. developed a vending machine called Redbox that could dispense DVDs for a buck a night at over forty-two thousand locations in the US. No employees and no rent made Redbox the final nail in the coffin for Blockbuster, which filed for bankruptcy protection in 2010. Blockbuster attempted to catch the waves that Redbox and Netflix had swamped them with, eventually offering movies by mail, streaming on the Internet (another innovation that Netflix had made work) and in vending machines, but by that time, it didn't have the energy or time to catch those waves. The remnants of the company were eventually sold to a satellite TV service, Dish Network, in 2011.

To avoid making a "Blockbuster" mistake, make sure that you keep up to date on the strength of your wave and constantly evaluate other waves that may be forming in your industry. Keep your eye on the horizon and an ear to the ground to stay up to date on developments that could present an opportunity or a threat. Listen to feedback from customers and to what customers of your competitors are saying. Listen to your competitors, too, and pay attention to market news and insights.

ACTION STEPS

1. List new initiatives you will bring to market and identify the ways you can fail safely.

2. List the competitors you have in the market, those who are on the bleeding edge of your industry.

3. Create and document contingencies for failures. Expect to have them, but plan to quarantine them, fast.

CONCLUSION

THE OTHER DAY, WHILE TRAVELLING THROUGH SCOTTSDALE, Arizona, I had dinner with Tomas Gorny, founder and CEO of Nextiva, a company that provides cloud-based phone systems for businesses. Tomas has launched companies out of his kitchen and brought them public, so he's no slouch in the entrepreneur department. Some would say he's lucky; I say he's a master of the SURGE.

Tomas owns several businesses. In 2008, one of those businesses was a web hosting company. By paying attention to the needs of those customers, Tomas noticed a trend: His customers were moving to cloud-based solutions for their websites. They were moving their office servers to the cloud and signing on to web-based storage, and Tomas saw this trend moving quickly. "I realized people saw the advantage of the cloud, and wondered what they would want to use the cloud for next," Tomas told me. That's when he came up with the idea to ride that wave by starting a company that offered cloud-based phone systems.

Tomas knew that people would soon put their entire phone systems on the web, but he also knew there would be a learning curve for their consumers. So, Nextiva catered to the movement. They developed extraordinary customer service, providing support so that their clients did not have to figure out how to make the shift they already wanted to make. And because Nextiva did not require sophisticated knowledge to master, it was easy for consumers to become early adopters.

Because it was first on the wave, and because it had the skills to ride that wave, Nextiva has had a meteoric rise. They just passed seventy-five million in annual revenue. And they are still riding.

SURGE is the method for rapid business growth. It is not for the faint of heart, and it is not for the entrepreneur who wants to stay comfortably in a lifestyle business. This is the method for growing fast with the least effort, albeit with the most skill.

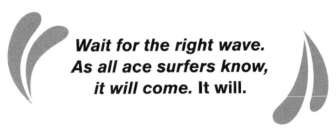

Wait for the right wave. As all ace surfers know, it will come. It will.

Let me be super clear: SURGE is not about predicting a trend in the marketplace. SURGE is not about making an educated guess on what might happen next in your market.

SURGE is a step-by-step strategy to spot a marketplace wave that has already formed, and then quickly position your business to ride that wave to industry domination.

During my dinner with Tomas, he told me that a billion-dollar competitor has been emailing him almost daily, trying to get him to sell Nextiva. Clearly, they see his company as dominant in their industry and they'd rather own the company than compete with it.

Tomas told me he recently replied to one of the emails, saying, "Thank you for your email, but I am not looking to buy your company right now. Let's stay in touch."

Yes, you read that right. Tomas told the company that wanted to buy Nextiva he wasn't ready to purchase *them*… yet. Tomas is riding the heck out of his wave, and even a big buyout won't distract him.

That's how powerful SURGE can be.

In the book *Switch*, Dan and Chip Heath talk about "lowering the bar." Most people try to raise the bar, to go all in. They get pumped up and push hard and then burn out fast. Instead, lower the bar. Take a small step. String together small wins.

My poker buddy Andy Groeneveld, a pilot for American Airlines, has a Dutch phrase he says from time to time, and it seems fit to share it with you now as you begin your SURGE journey: *Haar lopen ziin doet lopen.* Roughly translated, it means, "Those who come out revved up, burn out fast." Or, as my dad used to say at the kitchen table, "Fast runners are quick to walk."

Pick your niche and start studying it. Get really curious about it. Study its history and trends. Search online for "expert in (your niche)." If you find fewer than fifty companies, you should be thrilled, because there aren't too many competitors in the market. Chances are, you will find less than five companies. Or none. When you have those numbers, you have found a wave that is *begging* to be ridden.

Your next step is to begin the first phase in the SURGE process: Separate. You know how to do that, now. The key is willingness. Cyndi Thomason is the owner of bookskeep and a PFP. From the beginning, she was resistant to choosing just one niche. She didn't want to alienate *any* potential client.

Cyndi finally "gave in" and chose to focus on Amazon-based ecommerce businesses and devoted her marketing to that niche. Within sixty days of changing her focus, she got ten new clients. The work was easier, because she was catering to the same type of client and could implement repeatable systems. The marketing was easier, because she had a unified message, and the community she served promoted her from within. This simple shift changed Cyndi's perception of the process. Suddenly, she had confidence that she could apply SURGE to her business. (She also had proof that, even if her niche collapsed, she could recover fast by refocusing her identity.)

Take the first step in this book. Pick a niche, a narrow niche, and get really curious about it. Look for trends and history. Be patient. Wait for the right wave. As all ace surfers know, it will come. *It will.*

MORE BOOKS BY MIKE MICHALOWICZ

PROFIT FIRST

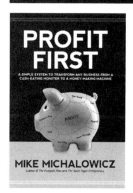

Sales − Profit = Expenses

You are about to discover the profoundly simple yet shockingly effective accounting plug-in that will transform your business from a cash eating monster into a money making machine. In *Profit First*, Mike Michalowicz explains why the GAAP accounting method is contrary to human nature, trapping entrepreneurs in the panic-driven cycle of operating check-to-check and reveals why this new method is the easiest and smartest way to ensure your business becomes wildly (and permanently) profitable from your very next deposit forward.

THE PUMPKIN PLAN

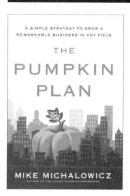

Who would have ever thought that the key to explosive entrepreneurial success was held by pumpkin farmers? Just as almost every pumpkin farmer grows ordinary Halloween carving pumpkins, most entrepreneurs grow ordinary, unremarkable businesses. Yet by tweaking their approach in small ways, farmers can grow giant, prize-winning pumpkins that get all the attention and press coverage. In *The Pumpkin Plan*, Mike Michalowicz reveals how applying the same few simple methods farmers use to grow colossal prize-winning pumpkins can lead entrepreneurs to grow colossally successful businesses.

THE TOILET PAPER ENTREPRENEUR

It is real. It is raw. It is entrepreneurship. "Never started a company before? Struggling with little or no cash? Have no experience, no baseline to judge your progress against? Thank God! You've got a shot at making this work." So says Mike Michalowicz, author of *The Toilet Paper Entrepreneur*, a business book that is so uniquely useful, so raw and entertaining, it reads like the brainchild of Steve Jobs and Chris Rock. Whether you're just starting out or have been at this for years, Mike's "get real" approach to business is a much needed swift kick in the pants.

All books are available at:
Amazon.com · Barnesandnoble.com · Audible.com · Itunes.com

For bulk purchases of 25 books or more, contact the Offices of Mike Michalowicz at 888-244-2843 x7002.

Want Mike to keynote your next event?

CONNECT WITH MIKE

Li Hayes ▪ Speaking Coordinator for Mike Michalowicz
888-244-2843 x7008 ▪ Li@MikeMichalowicz.com
MikeMichalowicz.com/Speaking